MY EARLY LIFE IN KENYA

(1971 – 1990)

by

SAMARA STEWART

Best wishes

Samara

2023

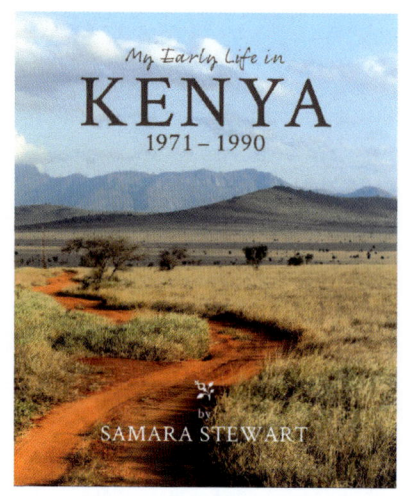

This book is for:

Amy, Ben and Lisa Stewart

Mollie and Morgan Matthews

Jacob and Ava Lowe

Their future offspring and many generations to come...

A few words from me, Samara...

An important lesson in life is you get one chance.
My Mum and Dad often said:
'Opportunities rarely present them self twice, take them when you can and you won't regret it'

They were not wrong.

This you will see I have done; I sincerely hope you've heard me say the same and share that with your children and beyond.

Love you all forever

Enjoy my story and explore when and where you can, take all opportunities, you will not lose.

Contents

Chapter One: Early days – Growing up 8
- Background & Scene setting • Early memories
- Safaris and typical camping trips • Cine film productions
- Ndololo campsite – Tsavo • Scorpion sting • Lions in the camp

Chapter Two: Home Life 20
- Water problems • Samara's Quarters/Hut • Security • Introduction to Pets
- Biggles – the African Grey Parrot • Ronnie – the Indian Rock python
- Car tax game • Learning to Drive • The coming of the rains; Flying ants and a free lunch!

Chapter Three: Ponies & Horses 34
- Molesworth family introduction to ponies • Ponies for Christmas
- Move to Langata • Hacks and Rides • Langata Pony Club • Drag Hunts
- Horses and Ponies over the years • Riding Clinics with Equestrian Stars
- Horse sickness jabs • Pony Club camp fun • Evacuation from Jamhuri Park
- Pony Club Camp 1982 • Out of Africa Film set • Timau Horse Show Fun

Chapter Four: The Banda Preparatory School 52
(September 1979 – December 1984)
- Assemblies/Break times/Lunchtimes • Sports • Aga Khan Swimming Galas
- School Crazes; Elastics and Marbles • Additional responsibilities
- School productions; Cats & The Boyfriend • Scottish Dancing

Chapter Five: Hillcrest Secondary School 62
(September 1984 – December 1989)
- General outline of school & location
- Extra-curricular activities; Spinning & Weaving, Choir & Sailing
- Car washing business venture • Fun in lessons! • 24hr Pedal Kart races
- Sports – hockey, squash, cross country running • Squash
- House Captain Responsibilities • End of Secondary School, End of an Era

Chapter Six: Hillcrest Expedition Club 72

- The Leaders • Mt Suswa introduction to caving • Lost in the Loitas
- Aberdare Mountains • Lukenya rock climbing
- Chyulu Hills 5-litres of engine oil • Origins of the Three Blind Jellyfish
- Mt Longonot & Hells Gate Navigation & Lion encounter
- Lightweight camping tactics & anecdotes - Mt Kenya trips
- Ndoto Mountains (Luggered in the NFD)
- Kilimanjaro: 21 to the Top – Closing Notes • List of Expeditions Logged

Chapter Seven: Flying 102

- Learning to fly • 1989: The seed is sown for the next phase of my life
- Navex Competitions • Flying Experiences 'Business pilot under supervision'

Chapter Eight: Adventures in my 'Gap Year' 114

- Collecting Jackie's A Level results
- Secretarial training & general experience gathering
- Lawrence safari in the Mara
- Flying Jackie & I to a 21st Party • Helping out on school expeditions
- Ewaso Nyiro & 'the Safari Surgeons" • Closing lines

Chapter Nine: End of a chapter in my life 126

- Dad's accident

Glossary 128

David and Diana Lowe

Preface

I have tried, by this book, to convey to the reader my idyllic life in Kenya from 1971 when I was born to when I left at the age of 19 for university and then to join the RAF.

With so many memories of happy days it has been difficult to be exact from year to year, so I offer this, not as a daily record of my growing up, but rather an account of my adventures and challenges along the way.

Of course, without the best parents in the world none of this would have happened.

So, to my parents, Diana and David Lowe I dedicate this book.

Acknowledgements

I would like to thank Ray Owen for his help and patience while writing this book. He was a source of great encouragement to me. Ray kept me focussed and proved to be a real Father figure taking the place of my Dad that I lost so early and tragically.

Also I would like to thank Claire Kendrick for her amazing design skills, advice in laying out the book and attention to detail putting in those finishing touches.

Finally, it has been great fun getting back in touch with friends from those days, sharing our memories of what we remember many of whom feature in the book.

<u>Map of Kenya</u> Numerous places mentioned throughout the text with regard to various safaris, expeditions, flying and horse shows.

Chapter One
EARLY DAYS GROWING UP

Background & Scene setting

Early memories

Safaris and typical camping trips

Cine film productions

Ndololo campsite – Tsavo

Scorpion sting

Lions in the camp

CHAPTER ONE

A bit about the background and set the scene

I WAS BORN IN KENYA IN 1971 TO wonderful parents who provided me with an idyllic childhood along with my two siblings, Jackie and David, whom I both loved and hated in equal measure, depending on my mood.

My father David Lowe, was a man of great drive and enterprise coupled with the fact that my mother had a great passion to go to Africa, made my childhood particularly happy and it was my father's spirit of adventure and his willingness to accept a challenge that brought them to East Africa.

My Dad was an excellent civil engineer and because of his job where he had to travel long distances, this gave him an excellent opportunity to expand and share his passion for flying. A 'bug' that I caught at a very early age. Kenya is a vast land and in the 70's when I was growing up a plane was the obvious means of transport for my father when he had to visit projects for which he was responsible. You can imagine that as a small girl, I quickly became fascinated by flying particularly when as a family we often went on trips with Dad.

Early Memories

My earliest memories of growing up were of being taken to kindergarten by Mum and our housemaid, Jane (ahyah), and my younger sister Jackie, often used to fight over who would be carried by Jane, strapped to her back with a kikoy, a fine cotton towel sized piece of material, as the local children were.

I promise you; this is much nicer than being in a pushchair. Another thing I clearly remember is sitting under the shade of the hibiscus tree with Jane gently checking my hair for the dreaded lice, a common school ailment. I often made up a story that I had them just so she could check, as I have always loved having my hair stroked.

For a short time, I attended St Christopher's School, near where we lived. It is here that I should say that school years in Kenya in those days ran from January to December. Although Mum had to drive me there. I remember very little about this school as it was decided to move us to The Banda Preparatory School,

Samara 9 months old

in Langata, the other side of town, for which we took the bus. The journey took about 45 minutes and there was many a dash to catch the bus, plus there was a school run system with the Mums so others were picked up enroute. With Mum being a maths teacher, I distinctly have memories of having to recite our times tables! She insisted the importance of needing to know them and she wasn't wrong.

We were great friends with Caroline and Sarah, the girls next door who were roughly the same age as my sister and I and we spent many hours and days playing in our garden in Muthaiga, about 5 kms from Nairobi (town). Our house was very close to the Muthiaga Country Club and we also spent many happy hours with Caroline and Sarah around the pool.

We often had monkeys in the trees at the bottom of the garden, which of course for us was normal. On one occasion Mum came out carrying a banana, which she proceeded to wave around, saying "I wonder if they know what a banana is?" well I can assure you they did, I still have a wonderful memory of them charging at my Mum who, taking fright, threw the banana as far away from her as possible, where the monkeys made a grab for it.

Mum and Dad had many friends which they made through work, flying and a very active social country club scene. As children we spent many hours at the Ruiru Sports Club playing tennis and exploring the grounds where the grownups rehearsed for

Jackie (nearly 1) Samara (nearly 3)

David, Jackie and Samara

Muthaiga Country Club Pool – David, Jackie, Sarah, Samara and Caroline

CHAPTER ONE

amateur theatricals. Often these would end up late at night with us kids fast asleep in the back of our Peugeot 504, of course bedding was always taken 'just in case'.

Jackie and I often got into trouble for squabbling and arguing which resulted our being banned to the bedroom with a stern "you just wait till your Dad comes home". We would wait with some little trepidation for Dad to arrive, but in truth, whilst the words were stern we really got away with murder! There was one occasion when having been sent to our room to wait I had a cunning plan to send Jackie out of the window to go and get some snacks from the kitchen. As she dropped to the ground and turned around, she saw Mum pushing baby David in the garden! Oops now we were REALLY in trouble!

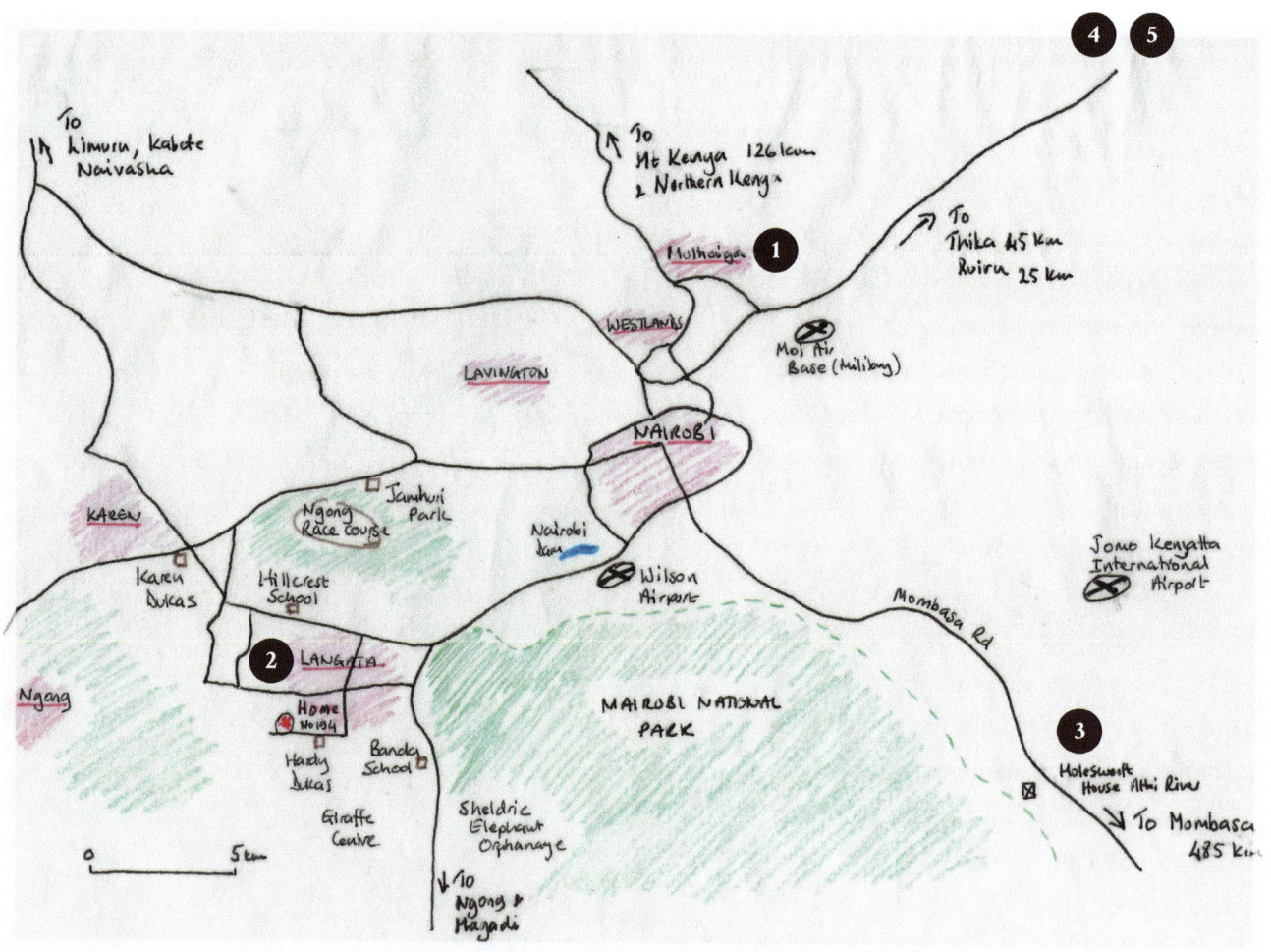

Map of general areas mentioned

1 - Muthaiga   2 - Langata   3 - Athi River   4 - Ruiru   5 - Thika

Samara & Jackie at the Coast – lovely and warm

Safaris and typical camping trips – early years

Many of our early safaris were with visiting Grandparents or Uncles and Aunts from the UK and from the Cine film footage and by what I can remember many of the holidays were spent in hotels either in the National Parks or at the Coast. This may well have been because we hadn't yet got into the true camping/real camping mode. We visited Voi Safari Lodge in Tsavo East and on down to the coast spending time at Diani Beach Hotel with the amazing silver sands and the lovely warm Indian Ocean. The sea was so warm it was like being in a hot bath, now you children know why I don't like swimming in the sea in England!

However, there are dangers of swimming in the Indian Ocean including a high possibility of stepping on a sea urchin. If that happened then the best way to get the spines out of your foot was to bandage a papaya fruit, also known as a pawpaw, skin to your foot which would soften the skin and cause the spine to be pulled out easier. We also did a lot of snorkelling to see the beautiful corals and fish in the warm water, and with the hot African sun we needed to wear pyjamas to stop us burning too badly because the water kept us cool, we did not notice the sun beating down on us.

As time progressed, we moved away from hotels and into Self Catering 'bandas' (cottage) in game parks. A banda is a small self-contained house with very basic facilities, a sleeping area, bathroom, cooking area and normally a veranda with a view overlooking a waterhole or a nice view. These were great

CHAPTER ONE

Kitani Self Catering Banda in Tsavo West National Park, everyone relaxing

Typical family camp set up with Taylor, Challoner and Lowe families

and then returned to Europe. However, we the Lowe family, were to prove otherwise and we were very much accepted into the well-established local community.

We had many safaris around Kenya, which included rock climbing, building dams in rivers to be able to swim and for the grownups to cool their beers in. I should point out to my children here and to any future grandchildren that camping in Kenya in those days was nothing like camping in England or France, so no washing blocks or toilet blocks or shops!! Every campsite was just a spot we 'found' in the bush that looked like a nice place, either found before or just happened upon. We had to take everything with us and when babies were involved there was always the running joke of did the 'nappy bucket' get put in! Once a site had been selected there were key jobs to be done as we often camped with two or three other families. Someone was dispatched to dig the 'long drop' (toilet) and always someone had to bring the 'thunder box', otherwise known as the 'thrown' to be put over the hole in the ground. If it was a luxury camping holiday there would be a tent we could put round it – otherwise it was just positioned well behind a tree or bush. If the Choo (Swahili for toilet) was in use there were various signals put into play – singing, or removal of the bog roll (toilet roll) from a nearby branch!

Then there was the 'catering area', complete with tent and kitchen. Everyone was

weekend retreats where you just booked, took your food and could do what you wanted not being restricted by hotel meal times. We spent many years using these facilities around all the National Parks and many a fun time was had.

Mum and Dad had lots of friends, many of whom were more long-term residents of Kenya and there was a running joke with our family that we were 'Two Year Wonders'! Many families came to Kenya on a 2-year contract either with a company or as a teacher responsible for providing various foods for the trip but it all went into the catering area.

The fire pit, was a key focal point for all campsites where much of the kettle boiling was done. A team of firewood gatherers was always organised once a campsite was selected and sleeping tents were each family's responsibility. Other important aspects were how to keep things that needed to be kept cold, cold or frozen for as long as possible, so woe betide anyone who entered a 'cool food box' without permission as it may defrost food or even worse, warm beers! Quite often campsites were located near water where beer and drinks could be kept cooler than the outside air temperature by being submersed in the water.

We camped with other families, over many weekends and in various areas of Kenya. This involved lots of different activities including rock climbing, walking, caving, mountain climbing, game viewing and just relaxing whilst we enjoyed the company of our friends

The river had been dammed to form a swimming area and somewhere to keep beers and campers cool.

and the great and varied countryside that Kenya has to offer.

The Molesworth family, Sue & Tony and their two daughters Leonie and Tammy, lived nearby and it was Sue who first introduced Jackie and I to pony riding. From this I developed my love of horse riding which played a large part of my growing up. Besides sharing an interest in ponies with Leonie and Tammy, Dad and Tony both loved flying.

As children, life for us was one round of adventure! Playing the "The Railway Children" at the Molesworth's house on the Athi Plains just above the Nairobi/Mombasa railway line, overlooking Nairobi National Park is just one example. I vividly remember going for rides, dodging the thorny acacias trees, on Bambi, Leonie's pony. Acacia trees were thorny and not very shady well suited to the arid and mainly dry climate of the African plains.

The campsite fire/oven – Samara and Gail keeping the fire going for the hot water

Molesworth's house at Athi Plains – Nairobi National Park below the railway line.

At weekends we spent many hours at the Aero Club of East Africa, based at Wilson Airport, which included being in the pool, on the swings and on the climbing frame. In the early years while Dad and Tony Molesworth flew and instructed students, it became quite a social scene. In later years, we spent many hours playing squash on the courts at the Aero Club and then for me in 1989 learning to fly at Pegasus Flyers, also at Wilson Airport and together with the Club was to become another important place in my growing up.

Cine Films

My Dad was a great enthusiast with his Cine camera, but in keeping with everything he did, it had to be done properly. So, after shooting lots of mini reels of cine film, Mum and Dad would shut themselves in their office and spend ages cutting, splicing, labelling and gluing together cine film, creating a wonderful series of historic films 'Lowefilms Productions'. They would then be sent to the UK to have a sound stripe put on them and then more time was spent finding music, writing scripts, rehearsing and finally recording the overlying sound! There are some wonderfully edited memories of our younger years in Kenya, including visits by Grandparents and relatives and safaris around Kenya in the 1970s and 1980s.

Recording the sound was a critical time as you only got one chance with the sound stripe on the film. In subsequent years Dad filmed an Imani school trip with Jim Taylor leading 4 school kids up Mt Kenya. This was then followed with a Hillcrest Secondary School expedition up Mt Kilimanjaro named '21 to the Top' in which both Jackie and I took part, more of this later in the Hillcrest Expedition Years section. The most fantastic record to have.

Ndololo Campsite stories Tsavo East over the years

The Tsavo National Parks, both East and West had from the very early days of Mum and Dad's time in Kenya been favourites of the Lowe family. The parks, although just on different sides of the road, were quite varied in character. Many of our early visits were more to Tsavo West where the terrain was more rugged and arid with volcanic hills and springs and views of Mt Kilimanjaro on clear days as compared to the more open and flat plains of Tsavo East.

A bit of background, Tsavo National Park is approximately the same size as Wales,

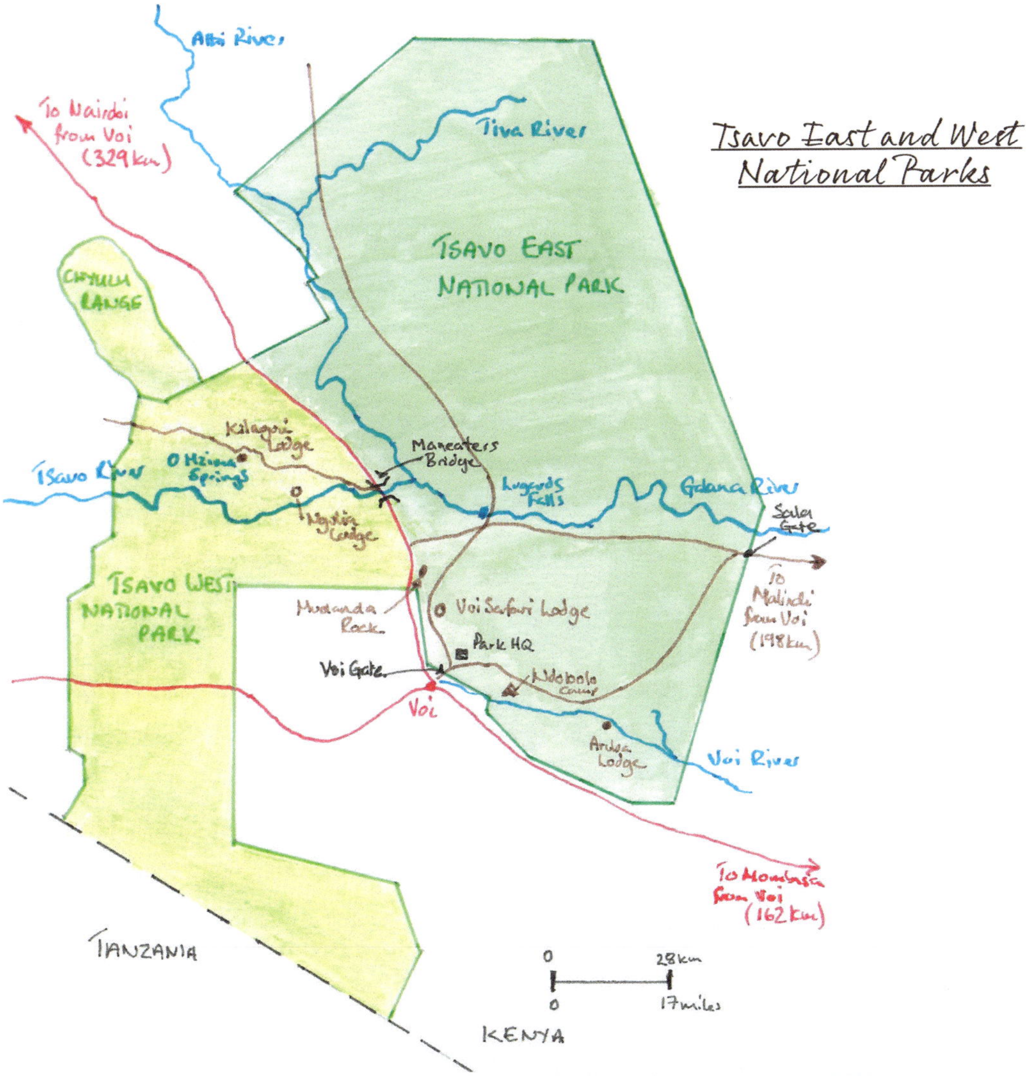

Tsavo East and West National Parks

20,000 km squared and is split into an East and West by the Nairobi - Mombasa road. To get to the Voi entrance of Tsavo East is about a 5-and-a-half-hour drive from Nairobi down the main road which despite being the main link between Kenya's main coastal port Mombasa and Nairobi the capital city it is still just a single carriage way and was very poorly maintained in those days.

Tsavo was known for its large herds of elephant and rhino but sadly due to poaching for Ivory the numbers dwindled almost to extinction in a very short space of time from the 70's and only just coming under control

Ndololo campsite from the air; river, beach, fire on beach & camp tree.

17

CHAPTER ONE

50 years later. The conservation of wildlife became a major focus for the Government both to save the species but also to protect one of the main sources of income and work through the Animal Tourist Industry. The 'war' against poaching and educating the world on not wanting to buy ivory became a major focus during the time of my growing up and I vividly remember the 'shoot to kill' policy coming into force in the Kenya Wildlife Service in a major effort to deter poachers.

Because of Dad's voluntary work training the Kenya Wildlife Service pilots on low-level anti-poaching flying missions, we spent many of our holidays in Tsavo East National Park in the 1980s. We camped at the Ndololo Campsite, a special campsite which was reserved for us by the Warden of the Park. Ndololo was located reasonably close to the Park Headquarters at Voi and the airstrip that Dad flew out of, which made it convenient for us both to get Dad to the airfield and then have the Datsun for us to explore the park.

Beautiful view of Tsavo East after the rains looking North East from Voi Safari Lodge

We normally set up camp for 10 days at a time and had a favourite spot under the shade of two trees near the river.

Depending on the time of year & how much rain there had been the riverbed varied from being totally dry to a river in full flow plus everything in between.

Even if it was dry, it attracted animals as they dig down to the water table, the elephants would dig down for water and all animals would take advantage. Some days we would spend just relaxing in the campsite, revising for exams, improving the campsite, watching birds or animals in general, reading books playing card or board games. Other days we might venture out on longer game drives often to Lugards falls and Mudanda rock and other places to explore and picnic. It was a huge area.

Every time we went it was different, the rains having shaped the roads differently,

Our campsite at Ndololo, home from home for 10 days

the animals behaving in different ways. We could tell if the poaching was bad as the elephants and rhinos were nervous. If it was dry there was more chance of seeing animals at watering holes, the wetter weather and thicker vegetation made it harder to spot things as they were dispersed because there was water available.

We were often in Tsavo East at the Ndololo campsite over Christmas and usually took different friends with us to share the experiences. Playing beach volley ball on the banks of the river, watching the fantastic night sky and listening to the amazing African night noises. Cicadas, lions grunting and trying to work out how far away they might be, hyena cackling and the noise of baboons in the trees nearby having family arguments. One never tires of all these sounds! There was one time when we had been telling campfire stories down on the river bank, I had decided to call it a night and was cleaning my teeth when 4 or 5 light brown shapes walked past. I didn't think anything of it, got into my tent only to find a short while later Jackie and friends were retreating from the fire to get into the cars as the brown shapes were lions and they decided to settle down and watch us! Enough to say we ended up having a very uncomfortable night sleeping in the cars!

On another occasion we were packing up camp after a long stay, I was wearing flip flops and suddenly felt a piercing pain in my big toe. I'd been stung by a scorpion! There was a bit of a scramble round, Jackie caught it in a jam jar and proceeded to identify it. I tried as best I could to remain calm as Mum bundled me in the car to take me to HQ. Jackie's conclusion was that it was only lethal to children or weak adults "Sam will be OK" she said. Inevitably by the time we got to the local hospital/medical centre in Voi Town the throbbing had begun to subside.

Samara stoking the campfire early morning

Diana & Samara at Mudanda Rock Tsavo East this was a wet year

Chapter Two
HOME LIFE

Water problems

Samara's Quarters/Hut

Security

Introduction to Pets

Biggles (African Grey Parrot)

Ronnie (Indian Rock Python)

Car tax game

Learning to drive

The coming of the rains;
flying ants and a free lunch!

CHAPTER TWO

ALONGSIDE OF THIS IDYLLIC childhood, there was of course the mundane day to day chore of living. For example, it is dark in Kenya at 6.30 every evening which obviously limited our outdoor activities. One downside of living where we were was the constant worry of security. Also, water shortages and sometimes food shortages such as sugar or flour, plus horse feed and hay. We just had to adapt and deal with whatever challenges came our way. Often these were caused by drought and plagues of 'armyworm.' These are a moth larva that look like they are marching when travelling to feeding sites destroying all vegetation as they go, consequently as a result causing shortages of crops. But there were many funny little things that were part of our daily lives, one being the race for the cream on the top of the milk on your breakfast in the mornings. Our milk was collected fresh from friends who had cows, completely unprocessed. Overnight the delicious cream would rise to the top and spooning this off onto your cereal, normally Weetabix, was a treat that was worth getting up early for. You can see where phrases like 'Early bird catches the worm' comes from!

Water problems

A re-occurring problem for us was the constant one of being short of water. Our house was at the top of a hill and so by the time the water reached us the pressure was very low with the result that more often than not we went without. For those, who are used to turning on a tap and having water appear, it may be difficult to understand the problems of not having water on demand actually presents. To illustrate how short water could be, we often had to share a bath, the nimblest being the first one in! Our house boasted many tanks and pumps in an effort to get water to the various rooms, stables and gardens that needed it urgently. Often Mum spent a lot of time taking our Datsun pickup, with the specially made water tank in the back, down to the local pumping station to collect water to fill up our tanks at home. The rain in Kenya essentially falls twice a year with April/May invariably being the wettest, followed by a short damp period in October. Between those times we were usually dry. When I explain that at one point, we had 8 horses each able to consume 6 gallons a day you will see the problem that my parents had. How they managed to do so still baffles me to this day.

We also had other members of our family, who luckily did not require much water, namely Biggles, our African Grey rescue parrot, and Ronnie, our Indian Rock python, who had been trained to eat dead mice. When Mum sent any of us to the freezer for ice, we had to be careful not to bring a dead mouse instead. Not good for cocktails!

Samara's Quarters/Hut

Between the house and the stables there was a small lodge which at one time had been a guest room for the previous owners. It contained a toilet and sink. I took a fancy to this and cleared it out one day, putting in a bed, my desk & a comfy chair. There I would sleep so as to be near my horses. It made a perfect little en-suite bedroom/study room for me.

I was very happy in my hideaway, but, one evening when my friend Amanda was staying over, we were lying in bed sharing stories when we noticed that we were being invaded by a stream of large black ants, coming in under the door. These are known at 'Siafu', Safari Ants, and could devour things in their way, so we retreated to the main house for the night. It always made me slightly wary after that of unwelcome visitors such as 'daddy long legs also known as crane flies, spiders but the geckos were always welcome as they feasted on the mosquitos.

Security

Security in general was an issue at that time in Kenya, so as a result most houses had gates and a security guard or night watchman was employed to patrol the grounds overnight and be available to open the gates. A security guard in Kenya is known as an "Askari". Ultimate Security was a Company that installed panic buttons in your house! If a button was pressed it alerted a team of security guards who wore protective helmets, had shields and were

Samara's hut in the garden

armed with batons, and were positioned in various places in the local area in a van. A team would arrive at your house within minutes of the button being pressed, the aim being to deter any unwanted intruders.

There was one particular Sunday we had friends' round for lunch and we were on the veranda having a BBQ when all of a sudden, we were surrounded by 15 or so helmeted guards brandishing their batons! We were somewhat surprised but on checking found that one of our younger guests had found a big red button which was SO tempting to push! A false alarm noted but at least we knew the system worked.

We did over the years need to use the alarm in earnest, and I remember one occasion distinctly. Within our house the bedroom area was separated from the lounge, dining room and kitchen area by a wooden locked door. One night we were woken by a loud crash. I looked out of my bedroom window which faced out onto the Veranda and a group of men had broken the glass in the sliding doors and were in the house. I ran down the corridor to get Mum and raise the others, Mum must have pressed for Ultimate but in the meantime the Mwivis (thieves) were throwing rocks at the door to our bedroom area. We are not sure whether this was to deter us coming out or whether they were trying to get into this area too. We certainly weren't heading that way to challenge them. It was quite a terrifying experience, but at least in this case we were all OK and so were our staff. The Ultimate Crew did come and from memory the burglars got away through the back of the plot with what they could carry. Certainly, a stark reminder of the need to be secure aware and safe.

In Kenya, all our windows had metal grills as a security measure. This was perfectly normal to us, but for visitors from the UK they must have thought we were like prisoners in our own homes. I guess now looking back it does appear that way, however, we never saw it that way.

Another thing about life in Kenya that was quite normal, was that we would just 'drop in' on friends for a cup of tea or coffee, as well as on horseback too. They were either in or not. Frequently a stop for afternoon tea drifted into 'Sundowners', the term used for an alcoholic drink enjoyed as the sun went down, and watching the nocturnal animals emerge. At one point we had a family of bush babies in the roof of our house for a while. Bush babies, for those unfamiliar with them, are like an African version of an Australian koala.

An introduction to Pets

Most people in Kenya had dogs mainly for security, but also as a family pet. I distinctly remember getting our first dog while we lived in Muthaiga. She was a pure-bred Doberman. We went to visit the litter of puppies and selected one and when she was old enough to live with us, we met her again in our garden. Dad asked us "what do you want to call her?" Our reply was "Emma", I have no idea why. He then said "and what about her middle name?" well this confused us and we really didn't understand why a dog needed a middle name! So not thinking I said "Just Emma" funnily enough that is what was then put on her papers and our new

Samara with Mum & "Emma, Just Emma" as a puppy

Doberman puppy was duly named 'Emma - Just Emma - Lowe'. I was about 7 so it must have been around 1978.

Dobermans are a very family orientated breed and so by nature extremely protective of family members. We soon learnt the need to warn any friends visiting to let us know they were coming first to avoid any less favourable welcomes. But given where we lived, having Emma was a great security boost both as an early warning and a deterrent to any unwanted visitors. A sign was displayed on the gate saying "Mbwa Kali" which translates as "Dangerous Dog".

Once we moved to Langata our menagerie of pets began to grow. We got another Doberman puppy a few years later called Tina, and then, through friends, who bred Jack Russels began to acquire smaller dogs too. The Jack Russels were not so easy to train! But they were excellent ratters and the funniest thing was they taught the Dobermans to want to chase rats too. However, as much as they tried, the Dobermans couldn't squeeze themselves into such small gaps. Sometimes it was like watching them in a 'Tom and Jerry' cartoon as they charged headlong at high speed towards a small gap a rat ran into!!

Biggles the African Grey Parrot

There was an occasion, in 1984, when a cargo plane had been impounded at Jomo Kenyatta International Airport and someone noticed it was full of baby chick African Grey parrots, which were being trafficked illegally. The load was confiscated and the KSPCA (Kenyan Society for the Protection of Cruelty to Animals) ended up with a

Ester, shamba girl and Peter holding Bodger

Biggles sitting on the door of his cage & Dad teaching him some phrases.

large number of young African Grey parrots which needed homes.

We decided we would get one. Well it was like adopting a child as an African Grey can live up to 70 years and also the KSPCA wanted to ensure you were going to home the parrot properly and not sell them on.

So, we got our African Grey and named him Biggles. Biggles very quickly became an important family member and as you may know parrots are renowned for being able to mimic sounds. So, we began to teach him various phrases and in order for a phrase to stick, you had to repeat it many times. Over the years Biggles has gained quite a repertoire. Which included the following phrases that I can remember:

"Biggles ready for take-off"

"God Save the Queen"

"Actung Spitfire"

"Hello Samara, Jambo Jackie, Good morning David"

"Is that nice? (every meal time indicating he wanted some!)"

"Where's my toast?"

"He could whistle 'Half a pound of tuppenny rice, 'pop' (said with a click) goes the weasel."

"Please tickle me."

He would call the dogs by name and whistle just like Peter, our House Boy calling the dogs for their lunch and he also did a very good imitation of a phone conversation or just general chit chat.

Sometimes he would muddle phrases and come out with funnies like 'God save Biggles'! He also had a habit of plucking his feathers which we can only imagine was a stress thing from his very early days but Mum and Dad were always worried in case we moved back to the UK. Biggles would obviously come with us and the quarantine department may think he had some nasty disease. So Dad taught him to say "I'm a feather plucker" sometimes he didn't always get it right causing much hilarity!

Biggles always loved a bit of whatever we were eating and often joined us at the table, we would carry him up to the table on our arm and then he would just wander round helping himself either off someone's plate or out of the bowls.

Biggles also liked some people more than others and like all animals he loved attention but you needed to know how to approach him to stroke him, if he wasn't in the mood his beak was very sharp. He never let Mum stroke him and almost actively went for her. We can only think it was because it was Mum that puffed doom powder over him once in an attempt to get rid of potential mites that were causing him to pluck his feathers.

He also loved chocolate and no matter how quietly you tried to unwrap chocolate he always knew and would get very cross if he didn't get a piece, clicking and snapping his cage, stomping his feet in a kind of way!

Biggles spent most of his day sitting on the door of his cage or on the top at the back just watching what was going on. Strangely on cold days he sat inside on one of his perches, not that it can have been much warmer in there! At bed time he goes in, the door gets pushed too and a blanket put over the cage. The job of the first person up was to take his blanket off open his door and say *"Good morning Biggles"*.

Ronnie the Indian Rock python

There was a day in 1987 when Dad came home and found David in the house with the pony Smokey Joe standing in the lounge! *"That's it he said, I'm going to get myself a snake, as every other pet seems to be in the house!"*

Well, that comment was like a red rag to a bull for Mum, and set her mind working. That Christmas we were in the UK and Mum and David departed for England. Soon after Jackie, Dad and I set off on the Hillcrest

Smokey Joe the pony in the lounge! And surprise slippers!

CHAPTER TWO

David (standing) with guests meeting Ronnie on our veranda

So unbeknown to Dad and the rest of us, Mum bought the snake and Dad opened up his beautifully wrapped shoe box on Christmas Day expecting a pair of slippers so it was a huge surprise to pull out a live 4foot long python - wow!!

I'm not quite sure how the name came about but we named it Ronnie, the Rock Python.

So, the next challenge was to get the new family member back to Kenya. You cannot just bring animals into the country without declaring them. So this meant we had to sort out and arrange all the import documentation, find how to comply with the rules regarding transporting a snake by air. Of course, with it being a reptile putting the snake in the hold of the aeroplane wasn't an option as he would have frozen so he needed to be in the main cabin. This was fine but the rules said it needed to be double bagged, in zipped bags, and in a plastic container with breathing holes. So, he was bagged in two zipped money bags and we bolted two seed trays together to create the other part, to meet with the IATA regulations.

The day arrived. The python was duly packed up and carefully loaded into a carry all and packed into the car with all the import and export paperwork ready. Our flight was a British Airways flight that connected on to somewhere in India. I distinctly remember the queue being particularly long and by the time we got to the front the check in lady

School expedition up Mt Kilimanjaro and we were to join them in the UK after our trip.

Mum, surprisingly had no joy, in finding somewhere to buy a pet snake in Kenya so she decided to get one in the UK instead, and so with the help of Aunty Liz found that Chester Zoo was selling some Indian Rock Pythons who had already been conditioned to eat dead prey, at this point in his life, frozen lab rats were his diet! Normally a boa constrictor would eat by suffocating their prey by coiling around it. Once crushed they then proceed to swallow their prey head first disengaging their jaw and taking it in.

was so pleased to see what she thought was a 'normal' family Dad didn't have the heart to tell her about the snake, it might have pushed her over the edge!

The next hurdle was the security check, Dad carefully placed his hand luggage on the conveyor belt at which point one of the security chaps roughly threw it on its side. We all visibly winced, as the bag went past the X-ray. Well from now on, all was going to be OK until clearing customs in Nairobi. We sat next to an American tourist on the plane who was so excited about her trip to Kenya but was worried about snakes. We assured her that you rarely saw snakes but had a little secret we would let her into once we had cleared customs in Nairobi! We certainly couldn't tell her about the one above her head or it may have created a panic on the plane! Suffice to say, clearing customs in Nairobi was fine and we shared our secret with our temporary American friend as we took her to her hotel! She remained remarkably calm all things considered when she heard what was in the bag next to her!

Now Ronnie was back in Langata he needed somewhere to live, but before we managed to get hold of a proper vivarium, he lived in my bedroom in a cardboard box with a light in it and a sheet of glass over the top. There were quite a few times as he got bigger and stronger that I would wake up and find Ronnie lying by my side, as he had pushed his way out under the glass and I was obviously a source of warmth!! Other times we would find he wasn't in his box and so everyone was sent to hunt for Ronnie which was often harder than it sounds.

It did get to a point soon after that we got a proper vivarium for him. I would mention at this point he was perfectly safe to handle and it was actually good to keep him handled. However, there was a technique to picking him up, approaching directly towards his head was not the way as this would appear to be a threat to him and he would go into defensive mode and strike. Pythons however are constrictors however and not poisonous!

With having a snake, we needed to learn about their needs. He would eat a frozen mouse in the early days, once every 2 weeks or so, the rate of digestion depending on

Ronnie by now a 2-man lift, supporting him important so as not to break his spine.

a number of factors such as warmth and activity. We got to understand when he was hungry as he would look like he was searching for food. Another interesting fact about snakes is that their skin doesn't grow with them so at various intervals he would need to slough, which means to shed his skin. When this process started his scales would become dull and the scale over his eye would become cloudy. Quite often and understandably, he could be quite agitated at this time as his vision was impaired so seeing danger was a problem. When he was ready to slough, he would bash his nose against a rock or something hard to break the front and then rub his body down the rock or along a branch or log to pull the skin off. If the skin came off cleanly it was an indication of a healthy snake, sometimes we had to soak him to help remove bits that hadn't come off smoothly to prevent infections.

Pythons can live for 30 years or so and just keep on growing and as they grow, they need larger food. Ronnie got too big to live in the house so Mum had a snake pit dug and covered in the garden and he must have lived to the age of 25 years or so, finally weighing in at 30 odd kilos and being about 30 foot long. By the end he was very heavy and it took two or three men to lift him and not damage his spine. The locals don't like snakes so the fact that we had one would have been general knowledge in the area which would have helped to deter any unwanted visitors.

Car Tax Game – Mum and knitting

The Datsun, our double cab pickup, was classed as a commercial vehicle and therefore needed taxing. This was usually very time consuming but Mum learnt to play the system. She would turn up at the council offices with plenty to keep her busy all day. She would normally arrive early, hand in her paperwork and then settle in a chair, sometimes she took her own, get out her flask of coffee and her knitting. She would put aside the day to that and looked forward to having the time to get some knitting done uninterrupted. However, the sight of Memsahib Lowe being settled for the day seemed to speed the process up and often her car was checked and taxed before she had

The Datsun pickup a multi-purpose vehicle doubling up as an artist's perch complete with an umbrella

hardly drank her coffee and she was sent on her way! Maybe the lesson here for all of us is to not look like you are in a hurry and beat them at their own game!

Learning to drive

As I grew older wanting to drive was something I was desperate to do. We were very lucky with often going into game parks, which allowed me to practice driving. Once in the park gates, I got into the driving seat and was in control for the Park trip. Another great opportunity to learn the skills of handling a car with no pressure of traffic only potholes, mud and animals.

Once I neared the age of being able to take a test, Mum and Dad booked me in for driving lessons at the AA school in Westlands, about a 30 minutes' drive from home. You needed to pass the theory exam before being booked in for a test, which had to be taken at the National Test Centre out near the Drive in Cinema the other side of Muthaiga.

I was failed on my first attempt due to an incorrect hand signal; but it was suggested a small payment might make it a pass! Well, No. This was not an option for me so I re-booked and passed it on my second attempt.

The coming of the rains; Flying ants and a free lunch.

One of my most evocative memories of Africa was the breaking of a long dry hot spell by the coming of the Rains. There are

Jacob, Lisa and Amy with their catch of flying ants, 2016. The cycle continues!

essentially two rainy, or wet, seasons in Kenya, April and October and in between the days are dry. Prior to the rains coming noticeable changes take place. The wild animals and birds somehow seem to sense that change is coming and they become more vocal. Kenya's landscape is dotted with termite mounds in which millions of ants busy themselves, awaiting the time when the pressure falls and the rains start.

This is the signal for an explosion of billions of flying ants to emerge from the ground to find a mate and start the next ant colony. The phenomenon usually, but not always happens in March or April when the long rains arrive. This emergence of flying ants is a time of great activity for rural Kenyans to whom these ants are a great delicacy. They, and now Europeans,

A flying ant: measures approx. 7cm wingspan and 1.5cm body length.

CHAPTER TWO

The veranda at Mum's house, the mural painted by Jackie

scoop up the ants and fry them in boiling oil or butter. Those tribes living around the shores of Lake Victoria actually collect sufficient to make 'Fly Burgers' which are 95% protein.

I know that eating ants is not something that everyone wants to do, but let me assure you that in our house we also considered them a delicacy. Fried in butter until they were crisp and served up in nibble dishes they taste just like peanuts and are not in any way distasteful.

You can imagine that for us as children it was great fun. This first rain was our cue to drop whatever we were doing, run outside with plastic bags and a butterfly net and collect as many of the flying ants as we could stuffing them into our bags which we kept tightly shut as we didn't want any escapees. The rain never felt cold, it was just so much

Front door is up the steps on the left

fun running around catching the ants. Once we had sufficient ants in our bags, we would go into the kitchen close the doors and tip out our bags which and then re-catch the ants most of which had now dropped their wings these were caught and put into tubs until we had as many as we could with no wings, some of them still crawling around. The next task was to fry them in butter, so Peter had prepared the frying pan complete with hot melted butter and we would decant the contents of our tubs into the pan. A very quick fry, not too long so they didn't burn and then out onto some kitchen paper to drain off any excess fat - then they were done and could be enjoyed hot or cold. They tasted like peanuts and quite crisp and crunchy.

Mum always made us help Peter tidy the kitchen of all the wings that were now almost impossible to sweep up, so, often for

The view from the veranda to the garden and field

a few days after you'd find another wing or two that had floated into a cupboard or onto a shelf and sometimes the odd ant that had escaped the pan! Once this rain had been it was always amazing to see how quickly the grass turned from the yellow crisp to having new soft green shoots.

Chapter Three
PONIES & HORSES

Molesworth family introduction to ponies

Ponies for Christmas

Move to Langata

Hacks and Rides

Langata Pony Club

Drag Hunts

Horses and Ponies over the years

Riding Clinics with Equestrian Stars

Horse sickness jabs

Pony Club camp fun

Evacuation from Jamhuri Park Pony Club Camp 1982

Out of Africa Film set

Timau Horse Show Fun

CHAPTER THREE

An introduction to Ponies with the Molesworth family

THE FIRST INTRODUCTION that Jackie and I had with ponies was with Sue Molesworth when we visited them out at their house on the Athi plains. They had a couple of ponies, Bambi being the little grey I remember most. Bambi had an enormous scar on her back rump from a time she lay on an adder but also starred in the film 'Flame Trees of Thika' and we spent many happy times riding her around the acacia thorn trees playing games of the 'Famous Five' with Leonie and Tammy Molesworth.

We then started having regular lessons at Mrs Goode's riding school on Friday afternoons after our school day had finished. Mrs Goode's was in Langata, not far from The Banda School so we missed the bus on these days as Mum took us to riding lessons.

Sue then invited us to various pony club sessions and even to go and take part in some of the Horse shows at Jamhuri Park, the premier Showground in Kenya. So, our first tasters of competition were in leading rein classes or clear rounds jumping and this certainly got us hooked into the equine world.

Our interest in ponies and the whole scene grew and expanded and we spent a lot of time over at the Molesworth's house in Langata, going to pony clubs and getting more involved, obviously to a point where it was time for change.

Ponies for Christmas

Then came Christmas 1981. Jackie and I got a pony each! But therein lies a story. No presents under the tree for us only an envelope each, which were marked with a muddy splodge. We had to work out the clue and with the help of very excited friends, Leonie and Tammy, we ended up outside at the stables and found two grey ponies inside; Alice in Wonderland for me and Smokey Joe for Jackie. We had one felt saddle between us and a very basic bridle for each pony. Here our real adventure with ponies and subsequently horses began in earnest. Mum, not really knowing one end of a horse from another threw herself wholeheartedly into this new

Bambi and I at Jamhuri Park with a clear round rosette, I was very pleased with myself.

world and became a very important cog in the Horse Association of Kenya (HAK) right up until the end of her life in 2016.

I have memories of rides without saddles, falling in the big ditch at the bottom of Milima Road as I bounced up and down on Alice's round tummy because Jackie had the saddle! The Pony Club on Sunday mornings was a regular occurrence, cleaning tack in preparation, learning all the bits for pony club tests, entering horse shows, falling often in the jumping competitions. Later the rules changed on how many times you could fall before being eliminated. We also took part in the numerous fancy dress parades at horse shows which was lots of fun and very creative.

Move to Langata

Once we had ponies of our own, we moved to a large bungalow in Langata, about 15 km from Nairobi. This move changed our lives. We were nearer to school, so no more bus journeys and a big garden with fields so we could have our ponies at home rather than at friends. We made many trips to the house into which we were moving as Dad completed the design work on the extension and managed the build.

The Penrose family lived at the top of Ushirika Road so only about half a kilometre from us. Avril and Helen had lots of horses and ponies and were also very involved in Langata Pony Club. I had regular riding lessons with

Picture of the house from the back garden. Visible is the lounge area and veranda (exposed at this point, it developed over the years)

Picture shows our house '194 Ushirika Road' from the front with the new extension on the right-hand side: dining room, lounge and kitchen.

Helen, who was a very good rider, she helped me enormously with learning to ride and then learning to jump with Alice.

Our trips to the UK now involved visits to horse shops to buy shoes and nails for the ponies, as those of quality were hard to come by in Kenya. Mum worked out what sizes we

CHAPTER THREE

Alice had quite a big jump in her, and learning to sit that especially on the sloped arena made for trickier landings, it was a great learning ground.

might need and how many to make them last until our next trip to the UK.

Hacks and Rides

As we grew up and got more confident our rides out on our ponies became more varied and exciting.

We had lots of fun hacking out locally with various friends with ponies who lived in houses nearby. Many of the hacks were around the roads which often had wide verges and some routes were particularly good with logs and culvert walls across people's drives so we were able to jump.

Some of our rides were more exciting, with some needing an adult to go with us, but later when we were older, we were able to go without a parent but always with two or more. The main reasons were for safety as it was more remote across the river, which meant a higher chance of us getting lost. Also from a security aspect it was safer as in those days mobile phones didn't exist so the fact there were two or more of us, someone could always get back to summon help if needed. There was always a high risk of meeting a giraffe, monkeys, bush buck or other wild animals which spooked the horses. I do remember falling off once, as my horse was frightened by a giraffe, and Avril, Helen's Mum, had to retrieve my horse for me so we could get back!

Amanda Boutwood was one of my closest friends, we did so much together as you will notice she features throughout the story of my growing up and has remained a very good friend throughout my life.

Amanda and I did some very long endurance rides complete with picnics and one I especially remember was out to the Ngong Hills. It was a real adventure finding our way out across the river and through the

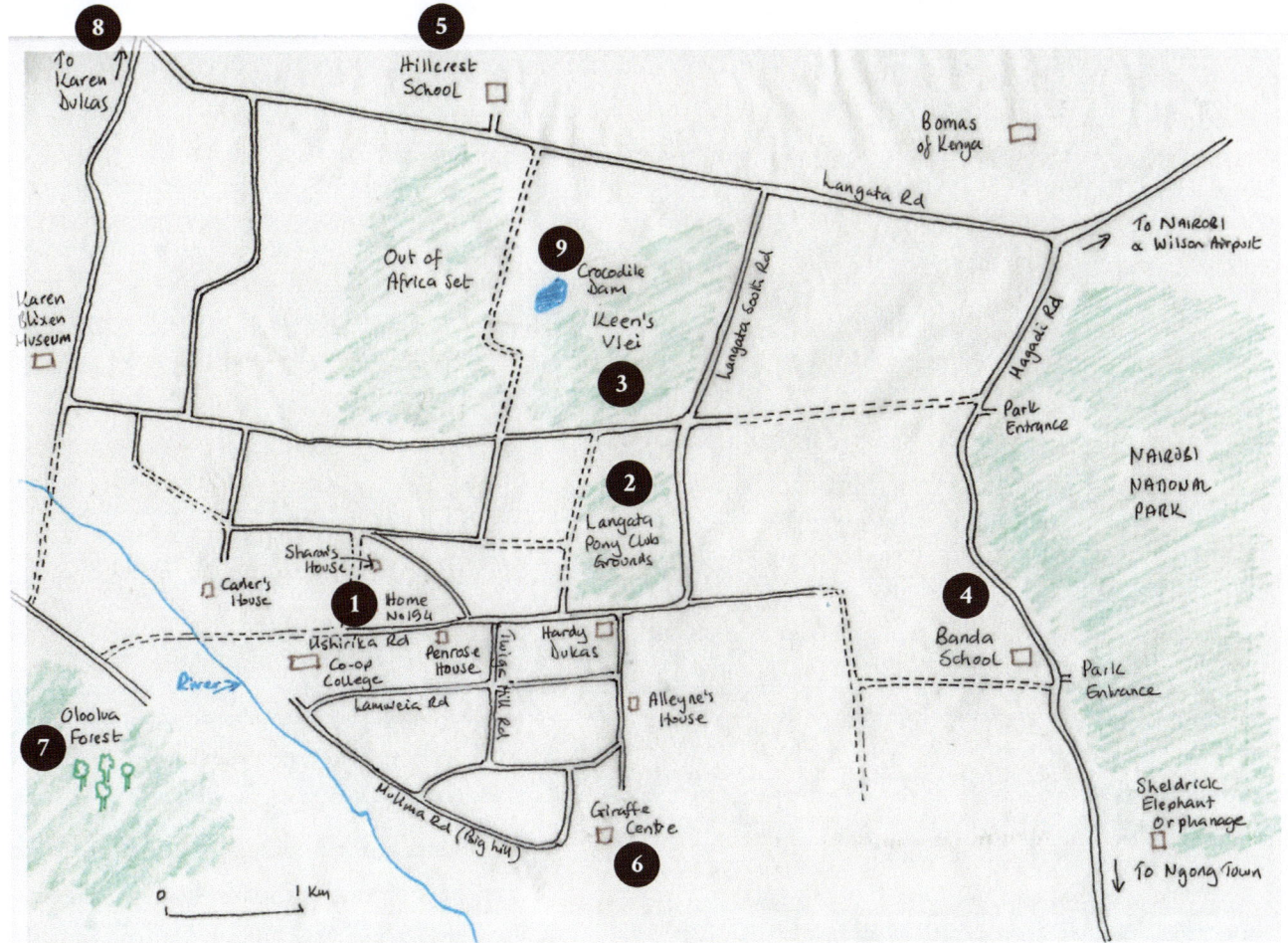

Map of locations visited and mentioned on horseback
1 – Home   2 – Langata Pony Club grounds   3 – Keen's Vlei   4 – Banda School   5 – Hillcrest Secondary School   6 – Giraffe Centre   7 – Oloolua Forest   8 – Karen Dukas   9 – Crocodile Dam

back end of Ngong town which was a very poor area with few police around. We were gone most of the day and again you need to remember there were no mobile phones and we didn't really know where we were going! We had rucksacks on our backs with our lunch and picnic blankets and also some nuts for the horses. We must have been gone 5 hours or so and certainly felt it by the end. It's a long time to be in the saddle, but lots of fun none-the-less.

When the rains came, many of our rides became flooded but that meant that the dam on Keen's Vlei (Vlei pronounced 'fley' is a big open area of grassland) filled up and we were able to take our ponies there to swim. It was SO much fun. We'd get there quite quickly then take the saddles off, hop on bareback, and take them in. If it was deep enough, they would actually swim but sometimes they would get in and just want to roll!! It was always funny when they got out and shook their bodies, like a wet dog. Staying on was a challenge when they were wet. Once tacked up, going home was often exciting and fast. I think we tried to dry the ponies off as much as possible so we

Samara on Alice in Wonderland Pony Club 1982

didn't' get into trouble with Mum.

There had been reports that a crocodile lived in the dam, which was further confirmed by an article in the local newspaper, I am not sure if that was to frighten and deter us, but we never saw it.

Langata Pony Club

We were members of Langata Pony Club and our grounds were just opposite Hardy Dukas (a convenience store) so only a 10 min ride from home. We were always split into our 'rides', which was dependent on what Pony Club test we were training for and on our ability. The day always started with an inspection which included cleanliness of the tack and pony and the turnout of both pony and rider.

From memory we got points out of 10 with the points going towards the 'team' you were part of. The rest of the morning would then be a mix of learning more information for the test and then skills of some sort, either some schooling, jumping, pony club games etc. We would stop for a drink and cakes at some point during the morning and I guess that the cakes/biscuits supplied, would normally have been home baked.

There was a lot of inter pony club rivalry, the other clubs being Nairobi Pony Club (based in Karen, 8 km (15-minute drive) in the other direction and Kabete Pony Club about 15km (50-minute drive) towards Limuru.

Drag hunts

I remember that when we were considered good enough if we wanted to we could join in the drag hunts. I recall distinctly the early

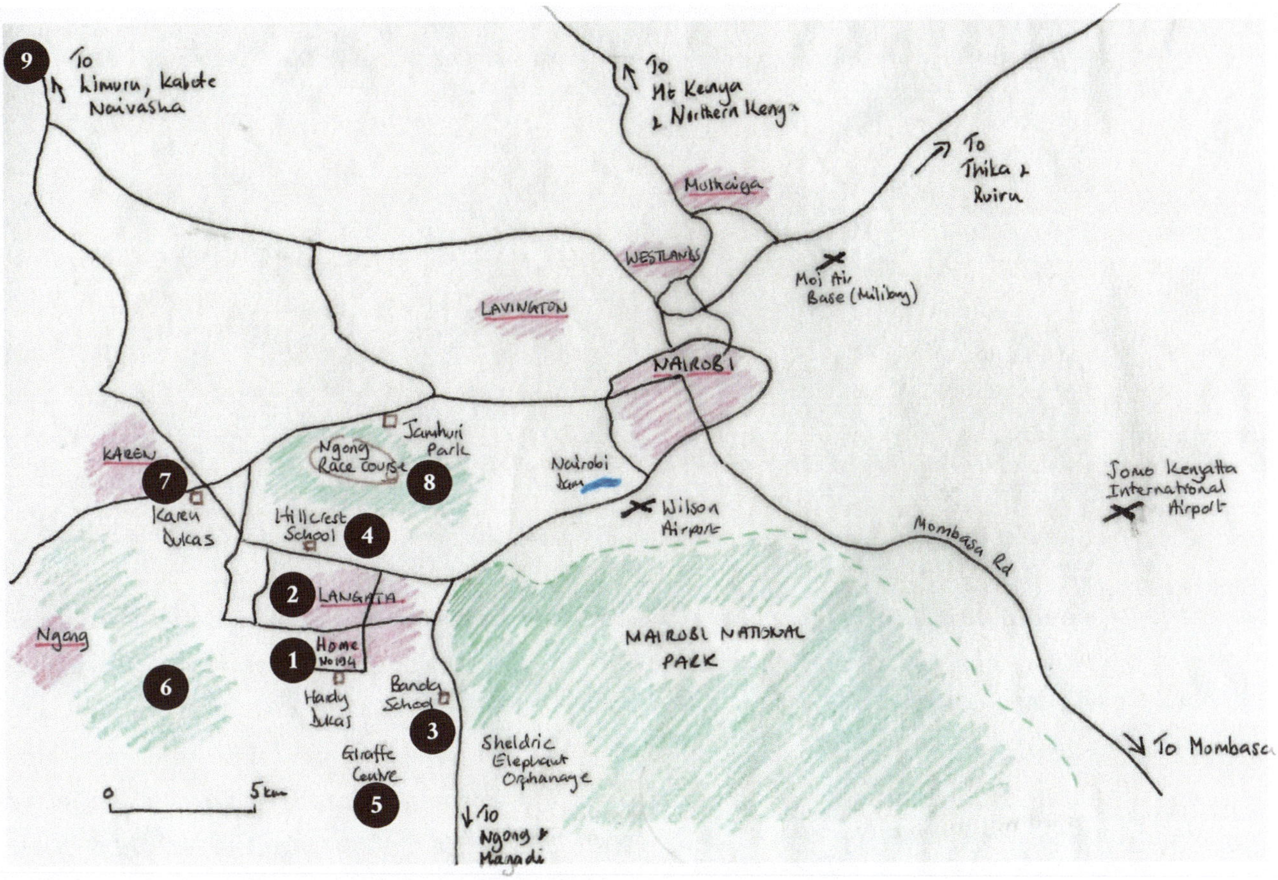

[Map of Nairobi area]

Locations frequented with the horses around Nairobi

1 – Home   2 – Langata   3 – Banda School   4 – Hillcrest Secondary School   5 – Giraffe Centre
6 – Oloolua Forest   7 – Karen Dukas   8 – Jamhuri Park/Ngong Racecourse   9 – Kabete direction

start, eager with anticipation, meeting up with Sharon on Victor who lived just behind us and all going down to the Keen's vlei where the hunt met. We were given a glass of sherry or something, as that was the 'done' thing, and then from there all I remember was hanging on for dear life as Alice and Victor just galloped with the rest. Our ponies were much smaller than those horses ridden by the adults' so we got splattered with flying mud and hoped the ponies would keep their footing and not fall down a mole hole and jump over anything that got in their way!

Hunting on Alice November 1982 Keens Vlei

Jackie on Smokey Joe and Samara on Sunset

We survived what can only be described as an exhilarating ride. A drag hunt is where a bag of scent is taken around the route before the hunt starts and this gives the hounds something to follow. The route can then be set as in Kenya there were no foxes to chase.

Over the years there were many opportunities to take part in these drag hunts which were organised for pony club camps as it was an excellent chance for the hounds to get a good run.

Horses and Ponies over the years

We were very fortunate to have not only our own ponies and horses but also the chance to ride out on others that we had on loan and that helped us gain valuable experience. I distinctly remember one afternoon after school mounting up for a nice end of the day ride round our field on Sunset, a horse belonging to the Penrose family. Sunset however, was quite an energetic horse and decided he wanted to have some fun so bolted with me around the field, completely out of control. I ended up with a ripped shirt and very shaken, and extremely worried parents!

He was a fairly mad horse and, as you can see, on the big side for me at that time but to be honest I was always up for a challenge! In the picture I you might well think I'm looking a little nervous of this rather big, exited horse, well you would be right! Jackie is looking slightly more relaxed on Smokey Joe.

Beano was the pony bought for me after Alice. He taught me such a lot. When he wanted to go it was serene but he had an extremely viscous buck, so learning to stay in the saddle was a skill in itself. If he didn't fancy doing cross-country, you'd be lucky to get to fence number 4 for example, but on other days he would fly round.

Dongoro was another youngster that we got, and this was a different challenge. We had to teach him almost everything from scratch although he had been backed, which meant he had been ridden with a saddle and bridle he was yet untrained. He was a lovely pony and again this was a whole new skill in teaching him from the start. So, no bad habits that had to be changed. I remember once having a high speed fall off him in a practice ring just before a show jumping class where I did a nose dive. For the rest of the show, I had a really attractive scab between my lip and nose that looked like a 'Hitler moustache'. Fortunately, it didn't need stitching and the show carried on!

Sorrel who was another horse I had was a real treat. A 14.3 hands high (how a horse or pony is measured) chestnut mare with white specks. She was a real jumper and a grade JA pony. This meant she was graded to jump only in the top competitions which essentially meant that all the jumps started at a higher height. From memory I think the first round of a show jumping for JA ponies was 3ft 3 inches and each round went up another 3 inches. Normally finishing in the 3rd round with all those who had had 2 clear rounds having to jump off against the clock with the fences now at 3ft 9 inches and a shortened course. Lots of fun especially on Sorrel and again a chance to learn new skills at a bigger height. She was a good all-rounder and performed well at cross country.

As it got light at 6.30am and dark at 6.30pm every day, the time for exercising ponies and horses was limited around school times, so I rode one pony before school and the second after. This was important so as to keep the horses and ponies fit, especially

Samara on Beano – 14.2 hands high gelding, quite a looker

when riding two or more at shows which was becoming very much the case. Morning rides were amazing as there were not many people about except those walking to work early, and often when riding across the vleis I was sitting above the low-lying ground mist, it was magical.

Samara's painting of Sorrel Feb 1987 in acrylic

CHAPTER THREE

Mum was much involved in assisting with various Horse Show Committees and I remember helping her to sort out the show entry forms with lists of ponies and horses entered into various classes. Also checking eligibility according to grading and ensuring the correct entry fee had been paid. This all had to be meticulously recorded otherwise you can imagine the furore it would have caused as any errors meant entries were either missed or entered into the wrong classes. Often ponies were used by different riders so when the show timetable was put together there was often a fairly complex matrix to ensure riders could take part in as many classes as possible, and all this took hours to do.

Riding to Jamhuri Park show ground was always a mass coordinated event in its own right, as the ride was about 12 kilometres on the most direct route from where we lived in Langata. This took us through areas which we were not used to, including the Ngong Forest and up past the Nairobi Racecourse, on the Ngong Road. Also, there were often more horses/ponies than riders so we had to lead as well as ride. As it was unfamiliar ground the horses often got excited, which made the ride more challenging without the added complication of leading one or even two extras.

By the time you were 16 years old, you had to move up to adult classes which you could do on a pony to start with, especially the likes of Sorrel, but actually to be competitive you needed a horse. So, buying a horse was another big step. Biddy Davies, one of my riding instructors offered me a young race horse of hers to try, his name was Kentucky Moon. She suggested I have him on trial for a couple of weeks to see how I got on. He was about 5 years old and had just raced. He was quite highly strung and very nervous of certain things and he hated radios, speakers and whips. I think he may have had a bad experience and where there were crowds, he would work himself into a muck sweat and foaming all over, but I loved him and wanted to bring him on so accepted the challenge and told Biddy I'd love to have him.

With Biddy's help I started to teach him. Kentucky Moon and I built up the most amazing trust between us. I never rode him with a whip and we slowly grew to know how each other worked. He tried for me and I loved him. Kentucky Moon, who

Jackie, David, Amanda and I with all our ponies heading off to a show just outside our gates.

I nicknamed 'Kentucky Baboon' was a 15.3 hand high thoroughbred chestnut gelding. He could really jump and although quite highly strung and excitable, but once I worked out how to contain his energy, he was absolutely superb. As we worked our way up through the grades in the various disciplines; such as dressage, show jumping and eventing we just got better and better together.

I never let anybody else ride Kentucky Moon as I didn't want that trust that had grown between us broken. We once spent hours trying to convince him that jumping over a log into water was OK and would not hurt him. Then when we started with novice cross country events, we would often have a stop and look at a fence, mainly ones with ditches, but I'd let him know it was OK then we would fly over it second time. The scores weren't great to start with but after a few events he never doubted me.

However I once had a bad fall off Kentucky Moon at the Pony Club practice cross country. I don't remember much about it, only what was told to me afterwards. Kentucky had taken off over a jump, unfortunately he caught the top pole, which being fixed caused him to somersault through the air. This threw me off and he landed on top of me but apparently, once he had righted himself, he came back to check I was OK. It seems I had come very close to snapping a critical bone in my neck and was very lucky in this instance. One of my nine lives, I guess.

Coming round after being unconscious on the sofa in our lounge, all I remember was a house full of people looking for Ronnie the snake who had escaped his vivarium again and seemingly not so worried about me! There followed numerous trips to a chiropractor to get my back clicked into place and going for X-rays on my neck. It was a while before I was able to get back on Kentucky mainly because I was so immobile; however, luckily for me all came right in the end.

Soon, we were winning jumping competitions, and starting to win and gain points in all disciplines, which meant we were moving up from Novice into Intermediate classes. When I left Kenya to go to University, my brother David continued the journey with Kentucky Moon, reaching the top level of eventing and becoming one of the top 4/5 show jumpers in Kenya. He was just an amazing horse.

Riding Clinics with Equestrian Stars

In Kenya we were very fortunate to have a really proactive team of instructors who invited prominent equestrian riders from overseas to come and deliver various training sessions. Among the celebrities we had Lucinda and David Green & Lorna Clarke to give eventing courses, various dressage riders and some showjumpers too. Often, they came just before a major event or show so we could put it all into practice.

Horse Sickness injections around shows

African Horse sickness is a viral condition that affects horses in different ways and as it is very deadly, we had to inject the horses and ponies to prevent this. They had to have two doses, three weeks apart from memory, and they were not able to do hard work as their hearts could be affected.

One of our friends Monica had vaccinated her horses but a dog fight broke out in her stable yard and it spooked one of her ponies who tried to break free only for the fence post, to which he was tethered, to be plucked from the ground. This so terrified the poor animal that it bolted back towards the field dragging the fence post. Once the commotion had died down a search was made for the pony but it was found stone dead! A warning to us all not to put their hearts under strain.

Once vaccinated the ponies were only allowed to do light work, just to try and maintain some level of fitness. Sometimes we timed it so we were away in the UK or on vacation and after the Horse of the Year Show which was in August.

Pony Club Camps

Pony club camps were great fun and I have fond memories from a very early age of going where we would camp out and had to do everything for oneself and the ponies. We went to some great locations on various people's farms around Kenya and they always posed a different challenge. I distinctly remember one camp, up near Nakuru at the Anti Stock Theft Unit (ASTU) base. This was a great location with some fabulous rides out but also the fun of learning with the ASTU chaps some of their tricks.

The ASTU always entered the main shows and were right up there in the competitive speed rounds on their amazing ponies that always looked far too small for them. And they also did amazing gymnastics displays which were awe inspiring, especially for us youngsters and captivating for the adults too.

Evacuation from Jamhuri Park Pony Club Camp 1982

Another camp in my very early days of pony clubbing and indeed which may have even been my very first was at Jamhuri Park, in August 1982. The show ground was eerily empty and as there were so few of us

The transport was quite basic and both the syces and horses endured some long journeys on bad roads!

Playing rounders at Pony Club Camp Sanctuary Farm Naivasha with a giraffe onlooking!

compared to a normal show, we all camped close together.

Unknown to us in camp a Coup had broken out in Nairobi. This was instigated by junior officers in the Kenyan Air Force who were joined by radical students from Nairobi University. As you can imagine chaos reigned for the first few hours until forces loyal to President Moi regained control. Nearly 300 people were killed in the clashes and a great deal of looting of shops took place. We were of course totally unaware of this as we were camped out at the Show Ground.

Word had got out and quickly spread amongst our parents who immediately jumped into action to come and get us together with our ponies. This was in the days before mobile phones so the only communication was via land lines and some families had radios. Action stations!

With so much chaos, it was difficult for them to find a safe way back to where we were whilst avoiding any shooting that was going on. We of course, fast asleep in our tents, knew nothing of this until we were woken up in the middle of the night by anxious parents urging us to hurry up but trying not to panic. For 10/11 year olds this was very exciting, as tents were taken down and we were bundled into cars. However, some children's parents lived quite a way from the Show Ground and were not able to get there to collect them, so they were taken back to home in Karen and Langata, where they stayed until they could be safely reunited.

With regard to our ponies, some were loaded into lorries which normally carried five ponies but we managed to squeeze in eight and others were ridden home by the syces (grooms).

Kentucky Moon water jump at Timau

The coup did not last long but was very frightening at the beginning. Nairobi came under curfew which essentially meant no travel after 6pm without official permission. If for example you had to travel for a medical emergency you were given an armed escort as there were many road blocks to be negotiated.

One interesting story that was told after life returned to normal was the tale of one of our more famous Kenyan residents, Lady Beryl Markham. She was known for having been the first pilot to fly solo across the Atlantic, non-stop from east to west, from Abingdon, southern England to Nova Scotia, Canada.

The story goes that she was on her way to lunch at the Muthaiga Club which was the other side of Nairobi, 20 or so kilometres away. On her journey she came to a road block but decided not to stop, so just put her foot down and drove through it. It is reliably reported that she made it to lunch but with a bullet hole in her windscreen!

Out of Africa Film set on horseback

The film 'Out of Africa' was filmed mainly on location in Kenya in 1985 with Meryl Streep and Robert Redford. The film was based on the story of Baroness Karen Blixen, a Danish lady who bought and managed a coffee plantation in Kenya in the 1920s. As a result, quite a few friends got involved in one way or another which was lots of fun and always caused intrigue and excitement. Mum and Sue Molesworth had got themselves involved in making accessories for the horses, and I distinctly remember all the webbing for the pieces they were making being dyed in the bath and then being stitched together. Sewing machines, thread and webbing everywhere.

One Sunday morning I went for a ride on Beano over the vlei and came across the 'Out of Africa' film set which had just been left following a shoot the day before. All the fresh fruit and vegetables from the market scene outside the station had just been left and was still there. I rode home as quickly as I could, and got everyone up and out we drove up there to have a look. It was an amazing sight to see and makes watching the film very interesting having seen it for real.

Timau Horse Show Fun

The Timau Horse Show was one of the best shows to go to. The location was at an altitude of 7,500 ft a good 2,000 ft above Nairobi and this made a considerable difference and impacted on performance and endurance. Organising and preparing ourselves for this event was in many respects a huge logistical challenge. They were all good shows but what stood out the most about this one was the fun we had camping, the parties were good and the location amazing! It was all held at the North Kenya Polo Ground and most of the competitors camped up there. The show jumping ring was on the polo ground, in front of the club house, the campsite to the left and the ponies all stabled on the other side of the polo ground. It was quite a logistical challenge as it ran over 3 days but we always tried to get up there 2 or 3 days early to ensure the horses were OK after a 6-hour lorry ride. We also needed to get the horses and ponies acclimatised as they were now being asked to do quite a lot at a considerably higher altitude. Exactly like humans the best way to acclimatise is to spend time at altitude.

Although we arrived a few days before the event started, we were not allowed to look at the Cross-country course until it was officially opened, but we did go on the most amazing rides. The best was going to the bottom of the airstrip which was adjacent to the showground and then just letting the horses gallop as fast as they could! It was great because the ground was soft, there was a much lower risk of holes. It had a slight slope and they were guaranteed to run out of puff before we got to the end so there was no worry about them running off with us onboard! Of course, back in Nairobi these horses and ponies would have been at peak fitness and full of energy.

CHAPTER THREE

Samara Jumping Kentucky Moon at Jamhuri Park

From the competition point of view the courses were amazing and the atmosphere electric. One of the events that was held each year was a sweepstake on the top grade Adult show jumping class. The riders were paraded in the club house and from memory we were auctioned off.

It made the support for the event amazing and the club house was alive with expectation. You were now not only riding for yourself but your new 'owner'. Lots of fun, nerve wracking but gave it that edge to push on. I vividly remember walking these courses and not being able to see over the jumps they were about 5 ft, same height as me and in order to have a chance of getting over them they needed to be approached at some speed.

Take off needed to be at the correct spot otherwise it might end in a bad fall and this was especially the case when it came to doubles or treble jump combinations. This particular competition was just pure show jumping held at the end of the gruelling three-day event which most of the same horses had also competed in.

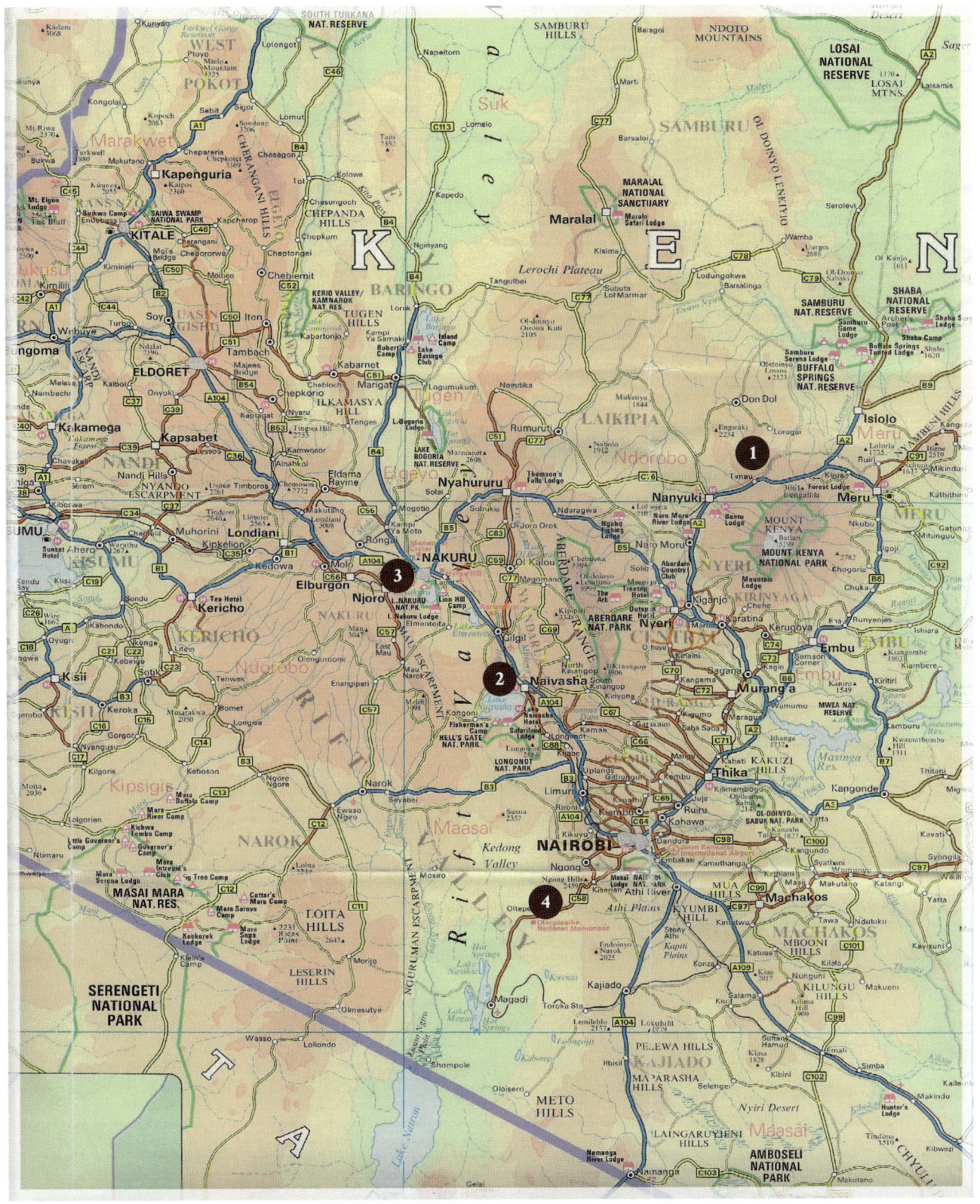

Locations of various shows and events
1-Timau   2-Naivasha   3-Nakuru   4-Ngong hills

Chapter Four
THE BANDA PREPARATORY SCHOOL
(September 1979 – December 1984)

Assemblies/breaktimes/lunchtimes
Sports
Aga Khan swimming gala
School Crazes (Elastics & Marbles)
Additional responsibilities
School productions (Cats & The Boyfriend)
Scottish Dancing

Banda School playing fields

1. School Hall   2. Snack shelter   3. Lunch Hall   4. Lower school classrooms
5. Upper school classrooms   6. Nairobi National Park   7. Sports fields
8. Swimming pool   9. Tennis Courts   10. Squash Courts

My EARLY YEARS, NEARLY 8 in total, were spent at the Banda Preparatory School. One vivid memory is the fun that we had participating in school plays and also it was here that my love of competitive sports developed and I revelled in the squash and swimming competitions. Our outdoor sport was not without its humour or indeed its danger, as from time to time there would be lions on our playing fields. Normally these would be harmless but one could never be too sure. From time to time, I would ride Beano, my pony, to school, Mum having gone ahead with Isayah, our syce (Swahili name for a groom). He would then walk the pony home, while I changed into my school uniform which Mum had brought in the car.

The Banda School is located opposite the Nairobi Game Park so the school run was always fun and as we drove down the road with the park on the left, we were always on the look-out for different animals. There was a particular clearing where we often saw buffalo & impala and occasionally, giraffes. We desperately wanted to spot lions but we

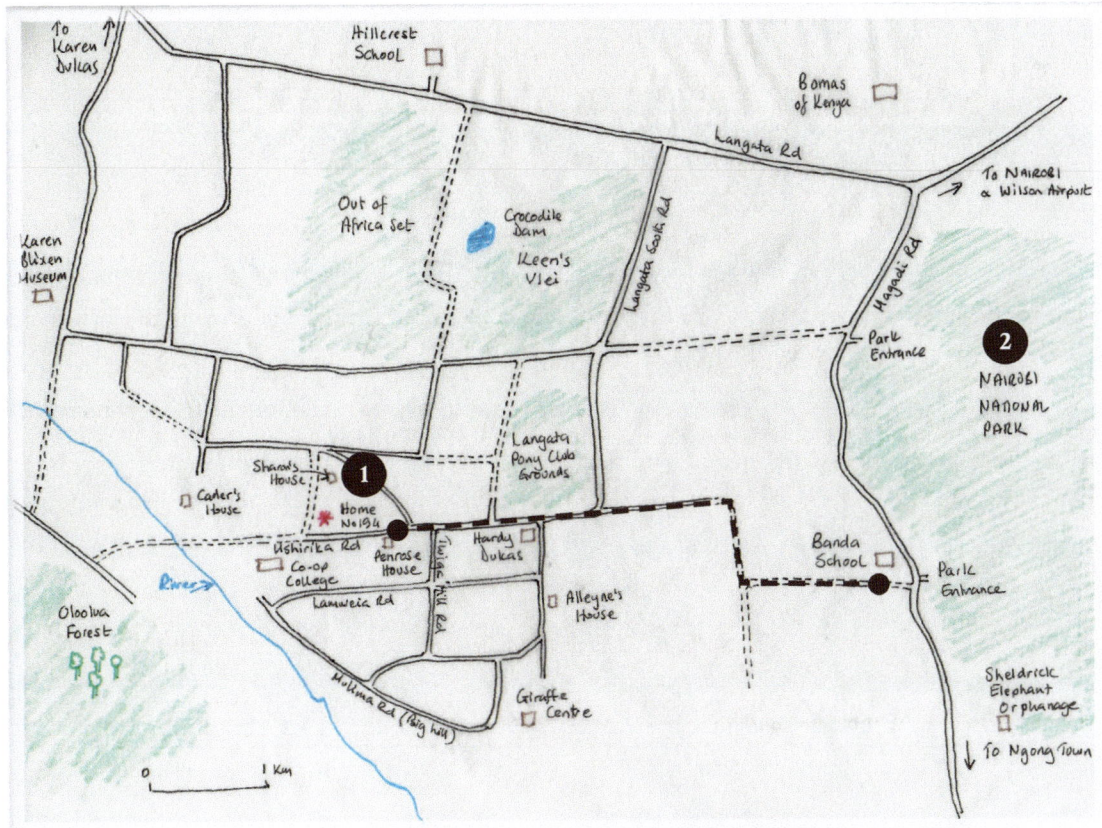

Opposite: Banda School playing fields, swimming pool, tennis courts and just beyond the playing field Nairobi National Park.

Map of the local area to home
1. Home   2. Nairobi National Park   Riding route to school ●- - - -●

never did. They may have been there but they spend most of their life lying down in the long grass and so they would have been well hidden. The Banda had its 50-year anniversary in 2016.

When I first joined Banda, the Headmaster was Mr Dalrymple followed by Mr Ian Wood who took over when the former left to go back to the UK. A large portion of the teachers came from England, stayed for a couple of years and then went back. For many it was a great opportunity to gain experience of Africa and some stayed on in Kenya and made it their home. I joined the Banda School in Lower III in September 1979 aged 8 years and after the first term was moved up to Middle III.

The system had 3 classes in each year group and they were graded as Upper, Middle and Lower. For each subject you were given a position in the class depending on how you had performed in all the subjects. School reports also included your position in class following tests and homework throughout the term and the end of term exam results were also ranked. If you were too strong for the class you moved up and if you were struggling you were moved down. Like most schools we did a full range of subjects; English, Maths, Science, French, History, Geography, Divinity, Latin, Music, Art and Games.

It was a fairly full day at school. To start with and for the first 2 years we came by bus from Westlands which was about a 40-minute journey from the other side of town. Once we moved to our house in Langata, however, the journey was much easier and only a 15- or 20-minute car journey (see the map). It was still past the game park and was much better than sitting on a hot bus.

Assemblies, breaktimes and lunchtimes

The school day always started with assembly in the main hall (see photo) so when the bell went, we formed an orderly and quiet queue outside our respective doors before we were marshalled in by the prefects. We all

Jackie and Samara in their Banda School uniform

had hymn books and the hymns of the day were listed on the wooden board by the stage and piano. We normally sang 2 or 3 hymns before the announcements. The teachers all sat at the back of the hall and we sat on the floor after the singing.

I distinctly remember break times where you would have to queue up for snacks and a drink of juice or water (photo shows snack shelter). The daily snacks were jam and peanut butter sandwiches plus a cup of juice. There were two queues; one for the bowl of jam sandwiches and one for the peanut butter. I liked to mix them so we would team up and get a friend to get one flavour while I got the other, then we would swap lids thus having our mix!

Lunch times were different. The dining/lunch hall was behind the lower school (see photo) a large open area with a concrete floor and brick pillars covered with a tiled roof. The lunch queue formed up in quad that was bounded by the staff room and school hall. We would have our hands inspected by prefects on the way in and if not clean enough then we were sent to wash them again and then had to re-join the back of the line. We very quickly learnt to be in the line with clean hands. Once everyone was seated someone was randomly nominated to stand and say a prayer for our food, which was then brought out and the teacher at the head of each table served lunch. Everyone ate school lunch and there were no choices. There were

Dinner Hall Banda School

certain rules and rosters for gathering up the plates etc and we always had pudding. My favourite was 'Kaptigat Mud' which was like a set chocolate custard. The name comes from Kaptigat an area upcountry known for its deep chocolate coloured mud.

Sports

The whole school had an hour of games at the end of the school day. We had amazing sports fields as you can see from the photo and the sports we played were rotated at each term. For the girls the first term of the year was hockey, second term netball and third term rounders. For the boys; hockey, rugby

The first XI hockey team: Samara seated front right.

The Aga Khan swimming pool ready for competition.

and cricket. Swimming was done as part of PE lessons, or as extracurricular activities at lunchtimes, the school having its own 25-meter pool. As with our lessons we all played in teams and the aspiration was to get into the first team for your age group so you could play in matches representing the school. There were lots of interschool competitions against other independent schools around Nairobi as well as up country.

Swimming Galas at the nearby Aga Khan School

Swimming galas at the Aga Khan school pool were always fun event. Queuing to get into the pool I distinctly remember the narrow path and steep steps which lead down to the pool itself. I was always the butterfly leg in team relays I was OK but

The team left to right Karen Keshavjee (front crawl), Kate Wilmer (backstroke), Sarah Hallows (breaststroke) and Samara Lowe (butterfly).

always thought everyone had an advantage as their height gave them quite a few extra inches in reaching the end of the pool. I only ever gained one medal as an individual and it was for breaststroke, I had made it into the final so we went off site for some lunch and when we returned, to my horror, from the top of the stairs I could see the finalists sitting in their chairs at the end of the pool ready. I hurtled down the stairs with a mix of emotions running through my mind, anger, frustration, nervousness and desperation to get there as I neared my chair, pulling off my T-shirt and discarding my shoes the starter called us to the poolside, blew the whistle and we were off. I just remember swimming as though I was being chased by crocodiles, no looking left or right, I'm not sure I even took a breath. The end result to my enormous surprise was that I had won gold at 25 meters breaststroke. In normal circumstances with lower levels of adrenalin I'm not sure this would have been the case.

There were also various interschool swimming competitions where we entered teams into the relay races. As you can see, I was a little smaller than the rest of the team but we did win the Medley relay in February 1981.

School 'crazes' – elastics & marbles

We had huge playing fields over which we were free to roam during break or at lunchtime, although with it being so hot, we often played whatever the craze of the time, under the shade of the trees. Especially as we knew we would be out playing games later and it would still be hot.

I never knew how a 'craze' started but the ones I definitely remember were 'elastics' where you had a big loop of elastic as in a giant elastic band and it needed 3 people. Two people to stand in the elastics making parallel lines. The elastics started around the ankles and the 3rd person then did a series of twists and turns in a routine. If there were no errors, the elastic progressed up to knee height then, hip height and so on, until the tricks could no longer be performed! That was a girl's game, they boys flicked the nuts that dropped off the trees using rubber bands!

The other craze was marbles. It was so popular, I think we even had a designated time which was known as the Marble Term for playing. Everyone had a bag of marbles and they came in different types, some more common than others. Common ones being cats' eyes, the rarer ones being 'cloudies', 'clearies' and 'bombies' plus numerous other variants. We would play behind one of the school blocks and along the back wall of the hall. It was a little bit like a market. You'd set up your marble pile to be won and then tout for players! Chanting phrases like "roll up roll up for clearies" or "get em while I got em" for example! You would have balanced a selection of marbles in a pyramid shape with some of the specials on the pile, then depending on what you had and how 'valuable' they were you would pace out a distance and mark the line in the dust with your foot. This was the line that anyone wanting to have a go had to stand behind to throw or roll from.

We created a myriad of rules to make it harder and how you could throw, there was always lots of haggling on what marbles you could throw. The deal generally was that if the roll missed your stack, you gained a marble, if it hit, they won it. It was such a compulsive and very competitive craze and there were top spots to get so there was always a mad dash after lunch to get to the best spot. We became very territorial!

Additional responsibilities

As we progressed up through the school, we got more involved and interested in the responsibilities we could take on. One of these jobs was being the school bell ringer. This was a huge old bell, most probably an old church bell, that was located in a flower bed along the school drive almost opposite the headmaster's office. This had to be rung to indicate the end of lessons, break and lunch. It was quite a task and I can't remember how it got allocated or whether you volunteered but you had to swing the bell with some gusto as it had to be heard right around the school.

School productions – 'Cats' & 'The Boyfriend' & Scottish Dancing

We had a very active music and theatrical side to the school and being part of school productions was always great fun what with rehearsals, costumes and then the big night itself. The ones I remember most was our production of the musical 'Cats', and then when I was in the 6th form, we did 'The Boyfriend'. I got a fairly major role in this one. Our costumes were made especially and we had lots of dancing lessons so we could all learn how to Charleston. Dad was working for a company that manufactured polystyrene at that point so he got very involved with helping to create the set. Mr Seaman the producer was over the moon and Mum got involved in helping to make costumes although Mrs Eames, another teacher with additional skills, designed them. The whole environment was fantastic and gave quite a buzz.

On the theme of dancing, Miss Gumoes used to teach Scottish Dancing which was great fun and I have fond memories of

The cast of The Boyfriend final scene, Samara & Graham front left

reeling around the school hall. It was an extra lunchtime activity and depending on numbers we would do reels of 8 or 16 which was quite a feat to coordinate all of us!

I finished off in Upper VIa, so the top class of the school age 13. At this point the options were to move to Hillcrest Secondary School or to board in schools in the UK. There were pros and cons to each so came to the UK and looked at numerous schools. This meant going for interviews, meeting the head teachers, viewing the school, looking at the prospectus. We visited probably 6 or 7 schools around England and Wales, some had been recommended as many Kenyan children had gone there, others were looked at as they were close to relatives which would make it easier to have support and somewhere to go at weekends. I cannot remember which school we decided on but I sat the Common

Above: Fifth form classrooms and main hall in the background

Left: Fourth form classrooms

Entrance exams, passed and was all set to go, and Mum was even sewing name tapes onto uniforms when all of a sudden Dad called a halt to it. He just said, this is silly we didn't have children to send them away, Samara will go to Hillcrest. So, this decision, made at the 11th hour, meant they had to arrange a place for me at Hillcrest, and a uniform was bought for there. Looking back, as far as I am concerned, it was the best decision Dad ever made on my behalf. So, in September 1984 I started at Hillcrest Secondary School.

Chapter Five

HILLCREST SECONDARY SCHOOL

(September 1984 – December 1989)

General outline of school & location

Extra-curricular activities: Spinning & weaving, choir & sailing

Car washing business venture

Fun in Lessons!

24 Hour Pedal Kart Races

Sports: hockey, squash, cross country running

Squash

House Captain Responsibilities

End of an Era

The front entrance of Hillcrest School, acacia trees in the quad.

General outline of school & location

HILLCREST SITS ON 10 hectares of land in the Karen area, about 15 kilometres from Nairobi. It was purpose built and started taking students in January 1975. By the early 80s Hillcrest had over 300 pupils of many nationalities. It provided education for children from the age of 13 in form 1 to the end of their A Levels form 7. The 'O' and 'A' level exams being set and marked by the University of Cambridge Syndicate.

Relative to our house in Langata the school was a 15-minute drive and the uniform was a navy-blue skirt with a sleeveless blue 'safari style' jacket and a white shirt. Once you got to the 6th form the shirt could be any plain colour but not too bright!

I moved to Hillcrest from the Banda in September 1984 aged 13. It was a last-minute change of mind of Mum and Dad's to keep me in Kenya and not send me to the UK to board as was quite a common choice for parents at

Aerial shot of Hillcrest School 1980s

1. Main Hall 2. Quad 3. Classrooms 4. Art block 5. Squash Courts 6. Swimming pool 7. tennis courts 8. Library & science labs 9. 6th Form classes and common room 10. playing fields

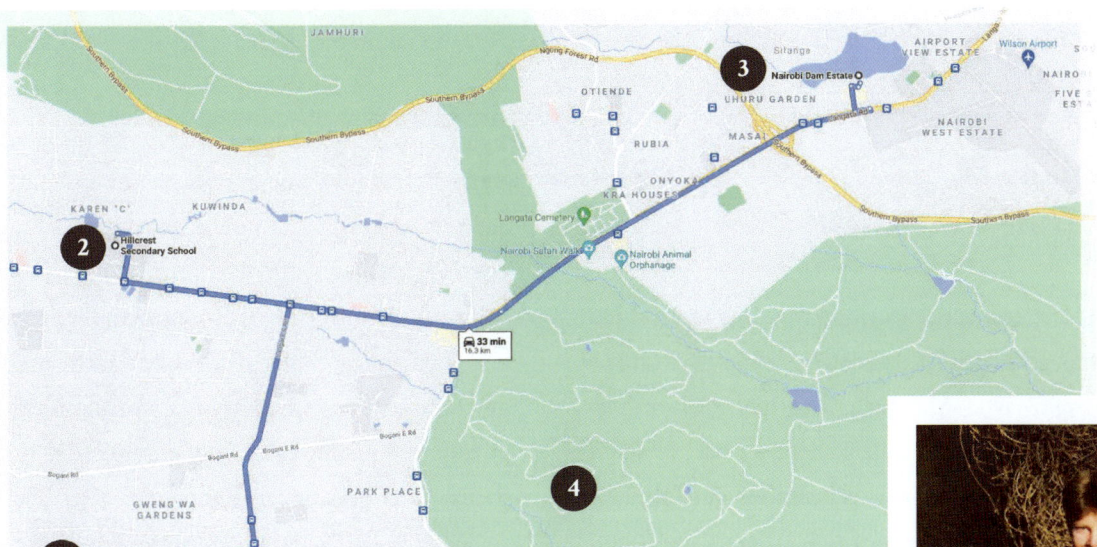

Route to Hillcrest from home
(The google map in 2021 shows it much more built up than it was in the 1980s)
1. Home   2. Hillcrest Secondary School
3. Nairobi Dam   4. Nairobi National Park

Samara and Jackie in Hillcrest Uniform with kikapu bags

the time. To my mind it was the best decision they ever made for me and hopefully some of the fun and stories that follow will help explain why.

In fact, in writing these memories down I found a paragraph in the prospectus which mentions what the school's aims are one of them being: "It is hoped that Hillcrest pupils will proceed to further education or the outside world with confidence and a willingness to play their part in the community in which they find themselves." Looking back at what I have managed to do and what I achieved I can modestly say that this has applied to me.

Interestingly, when I read back through my first report the opening remark from my form teacher was "Samara is perhaps a little too quiet". Well, my years at Hillcrest changed that.

Moving to a new school meant making a new set of friends who came from various other schools around Nairobi but also being with friends that I already knew through my riding.

Samara and Jackie in Hillcrest uniform David in his Banda Uniform. The dogs Bodger and Tina posing too.

Extra-Curricular Activities: Spinning and weaving club, Choir, Sailing

There was a spinning and weaving club which was something completely different and was run by Mrs Maynink who had a workshop at her house. I recall going there with a few others to learn the process of getting raw wool, sometimes very mucky with grass and having to brush it clean and then spinning it into yarn. We also learnt the process of dying the wool using natural materials which we were able to gather locally and then we did some weaving of the yarn.

There was also a choir run by Mr and Mrs Moss the music teachers and was great fun. We managed some really complex pieces and performed at various locations in Nairobi.

Our headmaster Mr Stevens was a keen sailor and conveniently for us Nairobi Dam was only 10 minutes down the road. Ian Munro, our French teacher also helped to run the Sailing Club which took place once a week. The school had a couple of Enterprise boats which were wooden sailing boats and good to learn on, but a nightmare if you capsized. The hull just filled with so much water that once the boat was righted it the only way to get back to the shore was to be towed by the rescue boat. As you can imagine it transpired that we mainly capsized at the furthest point away from the sailing club! A few years later the school invested in three Laser 1 dinghies which were much more learner friendly and easier to handle. Mr Stevens wanted to name the boats and as luck would have it, as we were very involved and keen on sailing, they were named: 'Samara', 'Amanda' and 'Helen'. We were extremely proud and felt we had made a real name for ourselves and he even commissioned us to paint the names on the boats.

There were various sailing competitions that we took part in. Sometimes they were in the middle of the school day and I had noted in my diary that Amanda and I came second in a competition and then had to get back to school for lunch and lessons. I also noted that we went down to the dam in our lunch break to sail, from time to time which was very convenient.

The new Laser 1 boats; Amanda, Samara and Michael rigging up at Nairobi Dam, Kibera in the background

Car washing business venture – Amanda and Samara

One day, Amanda and I decided that we could make money by operating a staff car wash at lunchtime. We even named our business "LowBout Ltd – Washing & Polishing Car Service" and set up on the slope behind the hall. There was a track that led down towards the kitchens which had access to a tap with a hosepipe. Staff would book in and move their cars onto the 'ramp' we would then get to work. Mr Munro was our most loyal customer but we had a few others who took advantage of our service. It was a bargain we thought at 20 Ksh (Kenya Shillings) for a car wash which equated to £1 in those days. We also decided to branch out into selling marmalade, lemon curd and tomato relish, but why we did still baffles me!

However, we had competition with Duncan Lindsay and his tuck shop. He had made an arrangement with the Rolf Schmidt, who ran an Italian pizza house and restaurant in Karen who agreed to supply Duncan with fresh doughnuts which proved very popular amongst both Staff and students.

Fun in Lessons

One of our French teachers was lovely and quite crazy in our eyes. Madame Solange Macellan was known to us as 'Madame'. Her mousy brown hair was always worn loosely in a big dishevelled bun on the top of her head and I distinctly remember her outrageously large earrings! She was quite a small lady. On occasion we were 'treated' to watching Tintin movies which was an adventure both in the film and the experience of watching it. The cine projector needed to be set up and this involved extension leads putting books under the projector until the correct angle was found to get the picture in a good spot. The cine film would often get stuck in the projector, the sound stopped and the next thing we noticed was the picture melting! Once Madame spotted this, she would leap into action stopping the projector, removing the melted film, snip out the burnt section using her nail scissors and then cello tape the film back together. Consequently, the Tintin movies got shorter and there were sections that had mysterious jumps in them!

Whilst Madame was busy muttering to herself in French, possibly swear words, it was a good opportunity for the odd person to slip out through a classroom window, come round and knock on the door. This created much muttering as it disrupted her film mending and then her surprise at letting a student back in that she never remembered excusing to go to the toilet! OK it was mischievous but fun too, and we never really got into trouble.

I guess that my French was never really my strong point and in my French O level oral exam, I was asked a question, thought about the answer, answered and was then told by the examiner – "Oui Samara, correct answer, wrong language", I had answered in Kiswahili!!

24 Hour Pedal Kart races

The 24 hr Pedal Kart Race around the Embakasi Race Track was an event not to be missed. It was run by the Round Table and was extremely well supported with over 30 kart teams being entered. This was such a great event and Hillcrest always entered 4 teams, some more serious than others. There were about 15 of us in a team, and our senior team tended to do very well in the overall ranking, coming 5th one year out of 32 karts with 330 laps in 24 hrs each lap being approximately 2km long.

It was fun, exhausting and exciting, especially at night round a track marked out by candles in brown paper bags with sand in the bottom! We had potholes to negotiate, sometimes punctures to change and chains to fix. At night one of the biggest hazards was the torch vibrating off the kart or a battery dying!

Often the teams were organised in shifts over the night phase to give half the team a good rest. Sleeping at night was a case of find a space in the tent, climb into your sleeping bag and try and get some 'shut eye', I can confirm

A hot change over in the pits – Hillcrest had 3 teams.

it was not comfortable and certainly when you got a shake to say it was your turn again it was a mixed feeling of "I'm too tired" verses "Yes let's get going again"!

Then there was the support team lead by Mrs Guest the home economics teacher who with her students would be on hand to provide nutritional support. This was essential for both the energy to keep going and morale.

Sports

During my time at Hillcrest, I took part in many sports at representative level; Squash, hockey, swimming, cross country running and representing the school at all levels. My love of hockey continued from the strong start made at Banda. I played in the first XI on the left wing and we usually had quite a full fixture list against the local schools with our biggest rivals being the Rift Valley Academy. Because the sport was so popular there were numerous school tours to the coast and one to Zimbabwe. I remember a coast tour, being an annual event for the first XI, and we travelled

Samara waiting at the start of a race, Ian Munro to push off and Amanda in support.

First XI Hockey Team – Coast Tour 1988 (Samara front row right hand side sitting)

Receiving my certificate for 2nd place at Greenacres School for Cross Country.

on the overnight train to Mombasa which was great fun. It was a 13-hour journey and there was always quite a high risk of it breaking down or there being an obstruction on the line as it went through Tsavo National Park, which always added to the excitement.

Cross country running was another sport at which I represented the school, and I distinctly remember going up to Limuru, to Greenacres School, about a 45-minute drive West of Karen. It was hard work running at the higher altitude of 6,000 ft above sea level. Hillcrest was at about 5,500 ft. I can assure you it made a difference and it was always much colder up in Limuru too.

Squash – where the love of it started

Squash wasn't really offered in PE it was more of an extra-curricular activity but Amanda and I were so keen to play we managed to convince Mrs MacDougal, the PE teacher, that we would be better at squash than tennis and so it was allowed.

We had sessions at school with John Mulwa the coach, and various members of staff but also went down to Parklands Club on Saturday mornings to join the junior coaching there.

As there were only two courts trying to get onto them could be a battle but as the saying goes possession is 9/10ths of the law. Amanda & I would rush down at lunch time to the courts, to try and get there before the boys and I remember having some 'heated discussions' on sharing court time. Often after a hot sweaty game of squash we would have a quick swim in the pool to cool off before afternoon classes started. This unsupervised activity would most certainly not be allowed these days!

If we lost out on the race to the courts, we entertained ourselves by climbing the wall on the back of the squash courts. It was built with knobbly bricks and made quite a good climbing wall but we were never sure if that was a deliberate design. However, it was fun and we challenged ourselves with harder and higher routes. Of course, none of this would

The Squash courts & back wall that we used to climb across

Amanda Boutwood, Tanya Warah and Samara Lowe

The Kenyan squash team touring Zimbabwe, Samara taking the picture. Ros Kyana back centre in the pink blouse heading up the team.

be allowed in these days as we were totally unsupervised and often came off and ended up with swollen and bruised joints!

The squash club played every Monday after school and had a team in the Milligan Cup league playing other squash clubs in the Nairobi area. These included teams from Kenya Airways, St Mary's and the YMCA and as these were against adults it was quite tough. We also played in inter-school tournaments at which we tended to do better.

Hillcrest School girls squash A team.

Outside school we also played in various squash tournaments around Nairobi and I played in a Ladies team with Mum for the Aero Club which was lots fun playing teams from other clubs. Playing in the junior tournaments led to Amanda and I being selected as part of a Kenyan team of 10 players to tour Zimbabwe and take part in the Zimbabwe Open in August 1987.

This was a wonderful experience and I clearly remember our first night staying at St George's Boarding School in a dormitory that was a bit like a hospital ward!

After our first night at the school, we were invited to stay with local families. On the whole they looked after us extremely well with Amanda and I staying with Mr & Mrs Fourie. We went to barbeques and the cinema and they generally involved us in their lives as temporary family members. This tended to be the norm as we would reciprocate when visiting teams came to Kenya and it is such a lovely way to get to know new people.

One of my other great friends during my time at Hillcrest, which I made through squash was Louise Leakey. Her father was the famous anthropologist and Louise and I

The Girls Dormitory at St Georges School in Zimbabwe.

always had really good games with the bonus that her house, situated on the edge of the Rift Valley near the Ngong Hills, had an open-air court. Although we didn't play there much, I still have great memories being at her house and staying over.

House Captain Responsibilities

As with most schools all the students are split into Houses. At Hillcrest these were Zeus, Odin and Thor. Zeus was my house its colour was yellow. Throughout the school year there were various interhouse competitions which included, cross country running, swimming, squash, debating, singing and really anything that might lend itself to a chance to compete. Some houses were renowned for being stronger at certain skill sets. Zeus tended to be stronger on the sports.

By the time I reached the senior school I was made a prefect and then the ultimate honour in my view, the girl's House Captain of Zeus.

Another enormous part of life at Hillcrest for me was the Expedition Club and as over the course of my years I took part in 24 expeditions around Kenya and Tanzania but this requires a chapter of its own.

End of Secondary School, End of an Era.

To mark the end of our school days at Hillcrest and to celebrate what we had achieved a Year 7 Leavers Ball was held which gave us, more practical girls, a chance to dress up. I went with Mum and bought a purple dress which became synonymous when worn as "Sam's off to a party"!

The leavers ball was held in the School Hall and included a Disco which was attended by both Staff and Students. There was also a buffet and you could buy alcoholic drinks.

The final assembly at school was quite emotional and as with tradition the Staff performed a review which was hilarious. We were then given our Expedition Awards before leaving speeches from departing staff. After that we the departing students line up to shake hands with all member of staff as a final farewell and I remember that I had a big lump in my throat.

Right: Amanda and I ready for the Ball

Chapter Six
EXPEDITION CLUB STORIES

The Leaders

Mt Suswa introduction to caving

Lost in the Loitas – Aberdare Mountains

Lukenya rock climbing – Chyulu Hills 5-litres of engine oil

Origins of the Three Blind Jellyfish

Mt Longonot & Hells Gate Navigation & Lion encounter

Lightweight camping tactics & anecdotes – Mt Kenya trips

Ndoto Mountains (Luggered in the NFD)

Kilimanjaro: 21 to the Top – Closing Notes

List of Expeditions Logged

A note here to my readers:
My time at Hillcrest besides academically preparing me for the world was punctuated by the various extra activities that I did, most notable of all of these were the various expeditions that I took part in. These included caving, rock climbing, walking and mountaineering so I hope you will indulge me if I describe a selection of these in detail as I recognise some terms may not be familiar to all.

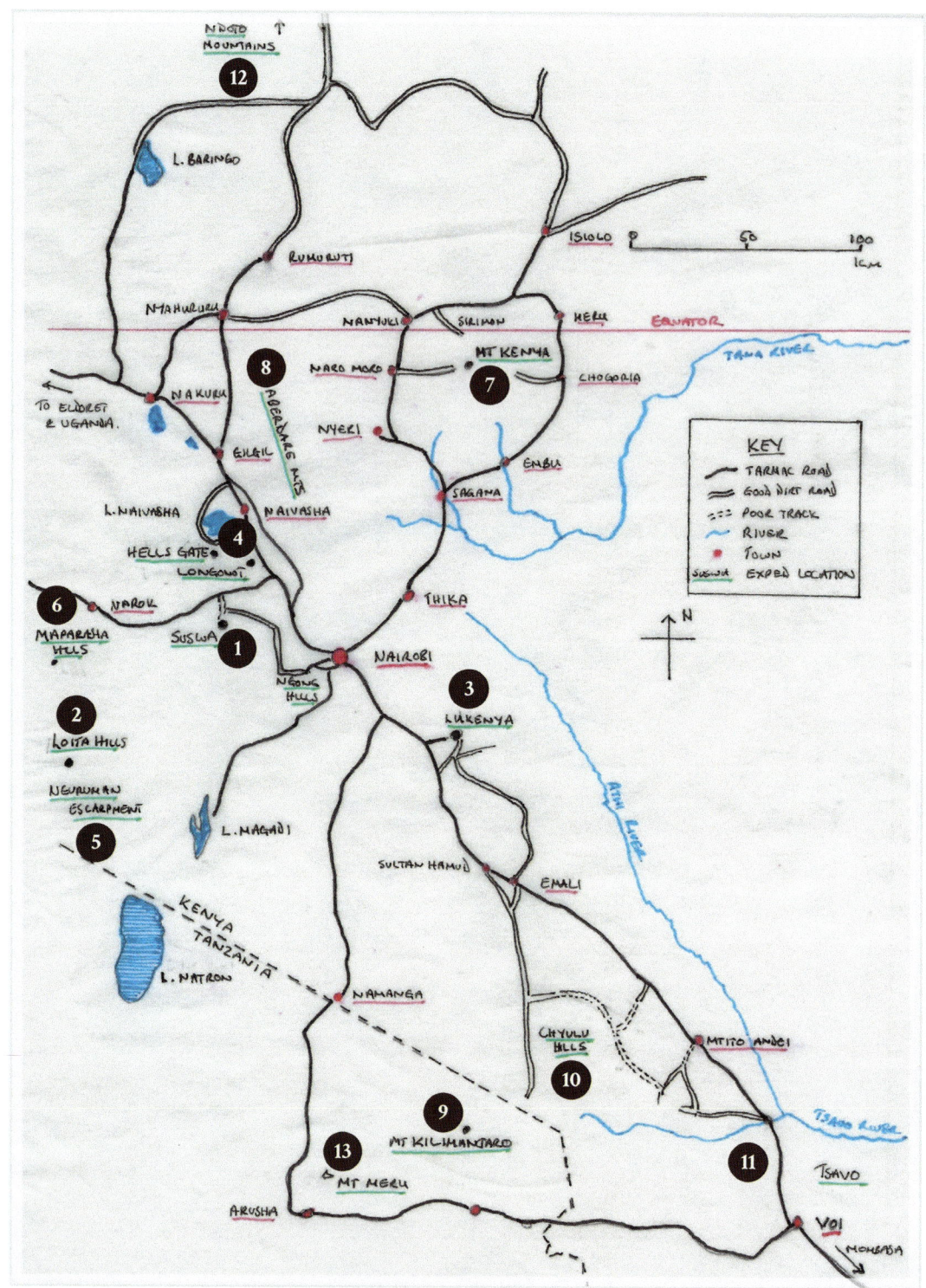

Map 1: Expedition locations

1. Mt Suswa   2. Loita Hills   3. Lukenya (rock climbing)   4. Longonot & Hells Gate
5. Ngurumans   6. Maparasha Hills   7. Mt Kenya   8. Abadare Mountains
9. Mt Killimanjaro   10. Chyulu Hills   11. Tsavo   12. Ndoto Mountains   13. Mt Meru

The Leaders

THE EXPEDITION CLUB WAS run by both our Chemistry teacher Mr Wielochowski and Mr Munro who taught French and it was a weekly afterschool club. The object was to learn map reading, first aid and the techniques of navigation so we could apply these skills and use them towards our Expedition Awards. During my time at Hillcrest there was a core of keen Expedition Club members who went on almost every expedition no matter how short or long! Then we had those who went occasionally for the experience, but everybody was required, as part of the Expedition Club, to keep a log book of our trips. As I write this book I laugh at the brevity and language used in my expedition log book entries. It has also been fun exchanging memories of our experiences with Amanda and Penny some 37 years later.

Mt Suswa – Introduction to Caving

My first expedition was caving at Mt Suswa in Sept 1985 (see map 1). We left on the Friday after school finished, driving to Mt Suswa. It is an extinct caldera in the Rift Valley with quite an extensive cave complex. In geographical terms a caldera is a crater formed when the mouth of the volcano collapses. The drive was about 2 hours and we arrived around 6.30pm just as it was getting dark. The first job was to set up camp, pitching our tents and getting a fire ready before all light faded. Out in the bush the only light other than the moon and stars was our torches.

There was no hanging around and as soon as the camp was up, we went out to do a cave appreciation walk into the 'Sheena Cave' 18a (see map 2). This is a cave where the roof had partially fallen in leaving a mound of large boulders and had root from the vegetation above dangling down into the space. For those of you who can remember movies like "Tarzan" or "Sheena Queen of the Jungle" it was typically that sort of entrance.

We headed off armed with our hand-held torches into this big collapsed hole. It was a relatively easy to walk down into it, climbing over boulders and once in the bottom there were fairly obvious tunnels leading off in different directions. Our first experience of guano, accumulated bat and bird excrement, which covered areas of the cave, as the roof of this large cavernous hole was a perfect roosting spot for the bats to "hang from". All in all, it was a super introduction to a cave system and we were

Example of the "Sheena" cave entrance

CHAPTER SIX

down there for about an hour?

Later, after supper, we were briefed on cave orienteering before being sent off to explore for ourselves. Another student and I spent from 10.30pm to midnight exploring the side caves as a pair. This was quite an experience, as it was pitch black and there many rocks to negotiate and we also needed to remember which was the way out. We kept our fingers crossed that our torch batteries would also last until we got back onto the surface. Then, of course, we had to remember where the campsite was located but in finding it, we were aided by the campfire as our guiding light. Exhausted after a day at school, a journey and the new experience of caving, we headed to bed to make sure that we were rested ready for the next day's activities.

Daylight gave the opportunity to practice orienteering which is essentially familiarizing ourselves with the ground around us, using a basic map (as shown) and a compass. There

A good example of two lava flow tunnels one on top of the other.

were plenty of cave entrances marked on the map but often tricky to find among the dry and thorny African shrub and acacia trees. We then got driven round to Hells Gate National Park, which lies directly North of Mt Suswa up the Rift Valley. As the crow flies it is only 35 km but to get there by road was a 3-hour drive, 80 km. At Hells Gate rock climbing up Fishers Tower a volcanic plug and abseiling before returning to school on Sunday afternoon – It was lots of fun and ended with a tired dirty group of children.

Shortly after we returned to Mt Suswa for the day to explore a few more caves, one of which Cave # 6a, was known fondly as "The Squeeze." This described the entry very well. It looked like a small hole between two rocks and you had to quite literally squeeze and wriggle your body through the gap, and then for me it was a precarious dangle and slide until your feet hit solid ground and then you were in a very dark cave. Despite the dry surface the inside was red earth and had a damp musty smell. It was also quite cool

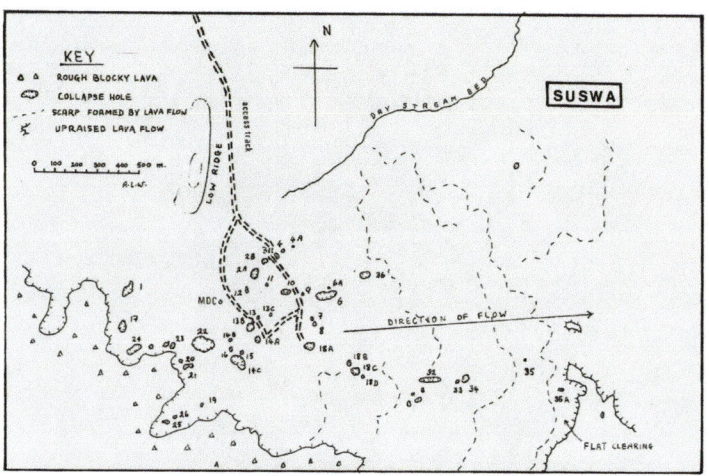

Map 2: Mt Suswa cave complex

relative to the temperature on the surface.

The caves were all different. One named 'Moby Dick' had lava flow tunnels, but the most fascinating cave of the day was #12 which had many interesting formations, one of which was called "the railway". This looked like railway tracks but instead of iron were made from lava ropes and also there were "bells" which were smooth chocolate coloured large balloon shaped formations that did 'ring' if tapped. You could almost picture the lava flowing through, cooling and making these shapes. The bells we imagined must have been formed when a large bubble of air expanded with the hot damp earth and like a balloon blowing up to create a bubble that cooled and solidified before it dropped, amazing. There were lava stalagmites and stalactites and a variety of secondary formations. It was very difficult to get pictures inside the caves so I hope the descriptions provide an image or you get a chance one day to explore them yourselves.

The Crystals in the cave were amazing.

It was great fun and we arrived back at school by 8.15pm covered in dirt. Normally this would not have been a problem except for the fact we had a water shortage so a nice deep bath to clean up was out of the question! Instead, we had a wash in about an inch of bathwater, after the others! Ugh!

Lost in the Loitas

By the third trip, we were considered 'ready' to try navigating at a higher level by heading off to the Loita Hills on the Western edge of the Rift Valley.

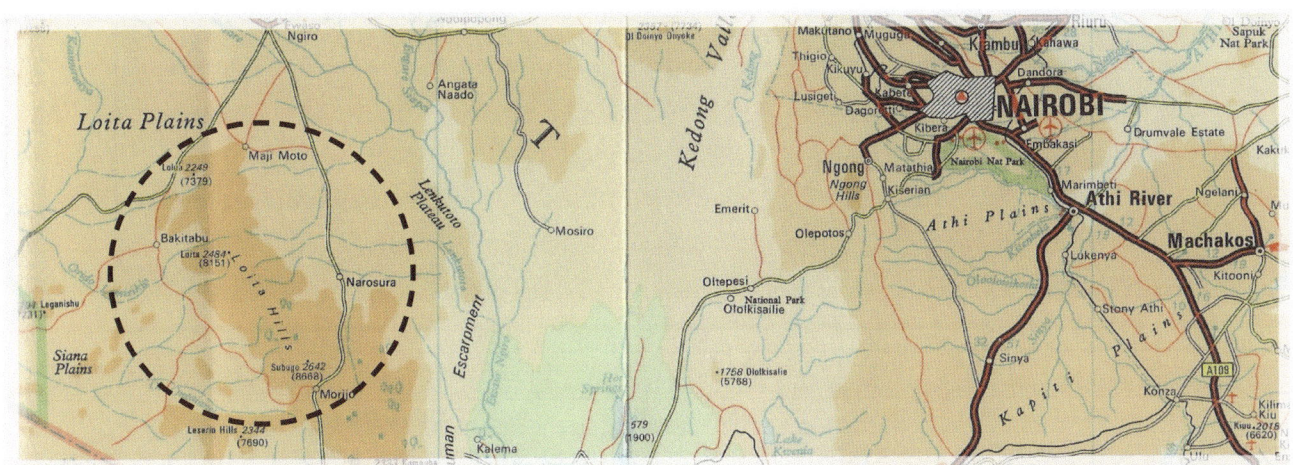

Map 3: Location map of the Loita Hills (South West of Nairobi)

CHAPTER SIX

We got to a campsite somewhere near to where we were due to start the next day at 9.30pm. We had 3 teachers and 15 children, and were split into groups of 5 per teacher. The plan was for us to take turns in navigating shorts sections to demonstrate our skills, each group departing at 5-minute intervals and to regroup at the next point. Saturday morning came and we all set off, I was in a group with Alan Arm.

Navigating through the dense undergrowth of the forest was extremely tough because for me the grass, bushes and scrub were up to head height. There were stinging nettles and bramble type plants all wanting to snare and catch you. There were no paths to speak of, just tracks where animals had flattened the bush. Normally when navigating, you would set your bearing by finding a feature on the horizon in the direction you needed to be heading and then set off knowing how long you roughly needed to walk for until you reached your next check point. The trouble was we were in a forest so the only thing you could aim for was another tree.

Off we went, pushing and picking our way through the thick undergrowth, chatting amongst ourselves, minding our own business when all of a sudden, a bush pig or giant forest hog charged at high speed out of the undergrowth right at us! Our startled shouts and screams had the desired effect as the pig did a sharp turn and dived off. I suspect the hog was as much startled by us as we were of it! It may have been a mother defending her babies or an older male that we had just got too close to. A wild animal's reaction is normally to get out of the way, but if you get too close, they go into defensive mode and charge or attack. This one had large tusks out of the side of its head, which it would have been very nasty if it had head butted us. I was at the front so would have taken the brunt of it.

Teachers were shuffled round and off we set once more. While this time groups 1 and 3 arrived at the second meeting point, group 2 never turned up. We spent the afternoon calling out for the lost group. Mr Munro and Mr Wielochowski searched to no avail. We camped in the clearing overnight and resumed the search on Sunday morning. The school bus was due to pick us up on Sunday afternoon on the other side of the hills, but by now we had lost time in searching, so reaching the bus with all of us was going to be difficult and finding the lost party was the priority.

The decision was for Mr Munro and remaining 10 children to return to the start point and Mr Wielochowski to run on to meet the bus and alert the school of the problem and get help to extend the search. The Mountain Rescue Team in Nairobi was alerted in the early hours of Monday morning, but in the meantime the school bus had arrived at our campsite, with food and the headmaster Mr Stevens who took us back to school.

In the meantime, helicopters, planes, walkers had all been summoned to search for the missing party. Finally, they were spotted from the air by a plane, and Rob Carr-Hartley flew a helicopter into a clearing to airlift them out. Whilst lifting off, the helicopter, got caught in a down draught causing it to crash land. So now we had a 'lost & found' group 2 and a crashed helicopter in the middle of the hills to deal with. Help included Maasai tribesmen and various volunteers and the group was eventually led back to base camp on the Tuesday and finally returned to Nairobi by lunchtime on Wednesday.

There was of course a story as to what had happened to the lost group with Mr Alan Arm. While being unaware of their exact location. Mr Arm had been stung in the throat by a bee and as his throat swelled up he began to choke and was unable to breathe. The bush was so dense and as they were upstream of the meeting point, our shouts were disorientating and being mimicked by birds, Mr Arm's condition deteriorated and he had to ram a towel down his throat to burst the abscess. They managed to find a clearing

Ian Munro with the group of 10 who needed to return to the starting point.

Samara, Marian, Louisa and Amanda Nicolls outside our Maasai tent.

on higher ground, but during their first night out, their camp was visited by a leopard, who fortunately only left tracks.

The next day food was rationed but water was needed so they made their way down to a stream when Mr Arm disturbed an unsuspecting buffalo who charged him and tossed him over some bushes onto some rocks. Amanda's shout deterred it from returning, fortunately the buffalo hit Mr

CHAPTER SIX

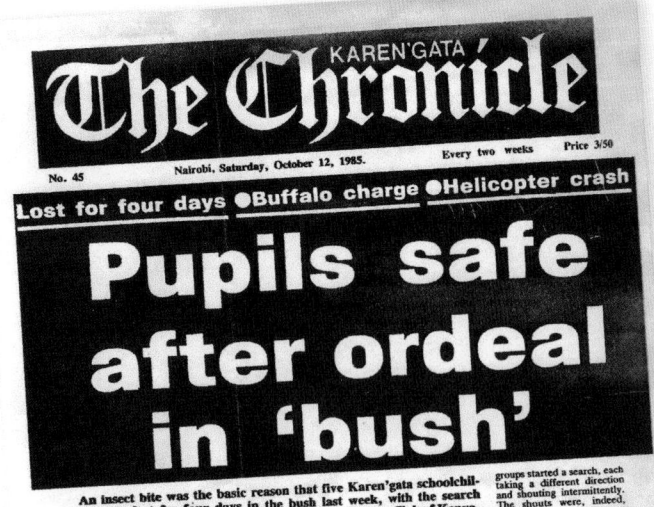

Arm on the back of his rucksack as he had half turned away so was not injured too badly. In their search for water, they found themselves trapped between two waterfalls and had to climb out. On reaching higher ground again and in a clearing the lost party heard aircraft searching for them, so they lit a fire to signal their location. All well in the end but an interesting life experience for all concerned. As you can imagine there were some very anxious parents and this was all in the days before mobile phones and therefore having to stick to the original plans made was essential. The parental debriefs were interesting and some suggested teachers carried guns or at least walkie talkies!

Aberdare Mountains trip

Just two weeks after the 'Lost in the Loita's' experience the Expedition Club was off to the Aberdare Mountain Range, which lies on the Eastern edge of the Rift Valley approximately 3 hours North of Nairobi. (see Map, located West of Mt Kenya) As we normally travelled by bus, it was pretty much guaranteed the bus would get stuck somewhere and we would have to do a lot of pushing and probably some road building. This trip was no exception and we had to start our walk with the Ranger/guide much sooner than expected.

The biggest memory from this trip was walking through 'elephant grass' which as it sounds consisted of extremely large tufts of grass so big it was like walking through a maze. The Aberdares are quite lush compared to much of Kenya, largely due to the high rainfall which fell. By the early afternoon, drizzle had set in followed shortly by mist and then full-on rain. The destination for the night was reached and we set up camp in the rain already wet and cold so it was quite miserable. Sleeping in a tent was tricky as there were 6 of us in a tent normally for 2 but we managed and soon warmed up. We kept ourselves occupied by eating biscuits and then we received the stove from the other tent at 1am. We heated up Penny's Mum's delicious homemade Chinese stew which was most welcome and after that we all slept well.

The bus we were expecting did not arrive so our walk was extended. By the time we got to our destination and were re-united with the bus, it was too late to depart plus the driver had also run out of petrol and cash. We stayed in a hut at the gate entrance to the park listening to lions chasing buffalo outside well into the night!

Lukenya – Rock climbing various trips

We made many school trips to Lukenya, a rocky outcrop about 40 km from Nairobi alongside the Mombasa Road. Quite easy to get to, it has a great range of rock-climbing routes from 'easy' to beyond 'Very severe', in climbing grades.

It was a wonderful learning ground for us, in how to go about being safe, learn the knots that are used and building our confidence. If you act

Map 4: Location of Aberdare Range and Mount Kenya North of Nairobi

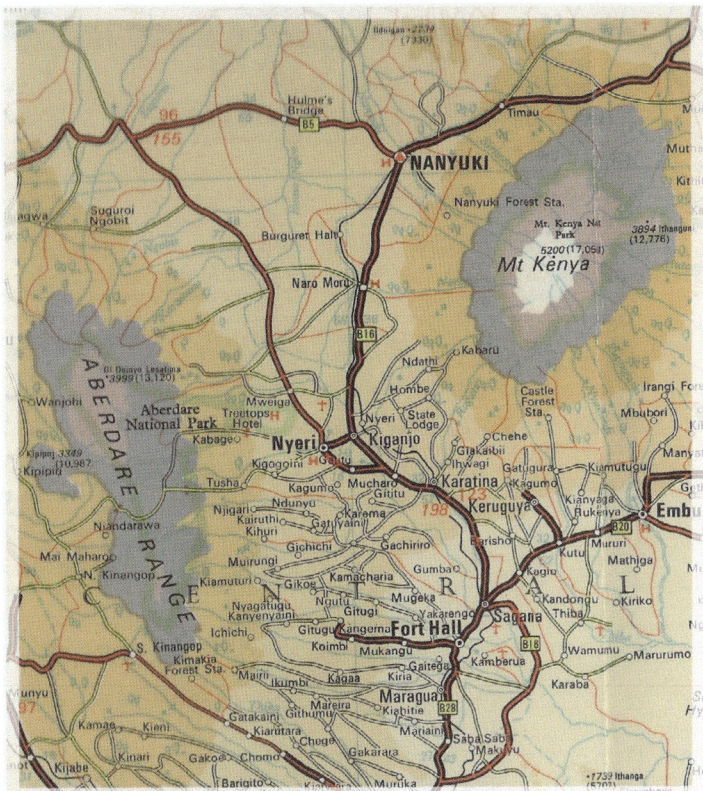

Rocky outcrops of Lukenya from the Mombasa Road

as a "belay", you are basically a secure point at the end of a rope while the climber negotiates difficult routes, so if they fall, they don't fall far. These points can be set up at the base of a rock or the top.

CHAPTER SIX

Water (oil) stop on the Chyulu Hills!

When climbing there is a whole host of specialist equipment to make it safer. As with any sport there is a basic level which includes; ropes, climbing harness & helmet. All sorts of extra equipment can be bought depending on the level at which you wish to climb but we were here to learn the basic techniques so as to be able to enjoy it. We were fortunate in Kenya that there were many enthusiasts happy to share their knowledge and experience so if you wanted to push the bounds further it was easy to do so.

Sometimes we stopped overnight, other times we would just go for the day

Over the years we climbed harder and harder routes and even had the confidence by the end of our time to be training the younger members and taking the lead on more challenging routes.

Chyulu Hills – 5 Litres of Engine Oil!

As mentioned before, many of our expeditions involved being dropped at one point and being collected at another at the end of the trip. Our expedition to the Chyulu Hills was another of these. The Chyulu Hills is a mountain range in South Eastern Kenya accessed off the Nairobi-Mombasa Road. It forms a 100-kilometre-long volcanic field in elongated NW-SE direction. Its highest peak is 2188 metres high and the Chyulu Hills National Park is one to visit if you like exploring caves. The Levithian tube is about 11 km long and one of the longest caves both in Kenya and Africa.

Due to their volcanic nature, there is very little water on the hills as the rock is so porous and, on this expedition, we all had to carry our own water supply. Bear in mind, it was also very hot and we would be walking most of the day and needing to keep hydrated. Well, the bus got us to the drop off point and we duly loaded our rucksacks making sure we each had our 5-litre container of water before the bus left us.

We all set off happily chatting and navigating as we went. A good distance into our walk we stopped for a much-needed water break and rest, it was then that Rachel, one of our school friends, pulled out her 5-litre container opened it up and to her shock, and our horror found she had picked up container of engine oil ! Well as you can imagine, she wasn't very popular, least of all with her team, who now between them, not only had to help carry this heavy container of oil, but also share their precious water with her during the trip! Suffice to say we all survived but even 30 years later when we met up for a school reunion it was a story no one had forgotten!

Origins of the Three Blind Jellyfish!

Getting to the locations on the expeditions always involved a journey in the school bus. This was no ordinary bus! It was like a van with windows and bench seats down each side and a big open gap down the middle. Certainly, this wouldn't pass the health and safety requirements of transporting children these days. Not a seat belt in sight! All the bags/rucksacks were either loose in the middle or they were strapped to the roof rack. In African terms in true 'Matatu' style. A Matatu is a local taxi/bus service where it used to be the case of squeeze as many passengers as possible into the van! You'll be pleased to hear by 2004 matatus became licenced and could only carry as many passengers as they had seats.

However, the point I am coming to in a roundabout fashion is that the journeys were often long and uncomfortable so we had to provide our own entertainment which was very much part of the fun. Lots of chat, singing and games made the time pass quicker. Amanda, Penny and I had a few songs up our sleeves and one that became a regular, mainly because it was annoying to most of our passengers was "Three Blind Jellyfish", we particularly liked it as we could do the actions. Also there was a chance for audience participation and we took every opportunity to sing it. I won't write the whole song out but the words went something like this ....

Sung: *"Three blind jellyfish, three blind jellyfish, three blind jellyfish sitting on a rock"*

Said: *"and a wave came & knocked one off"* and everyone says "Oooh" (one of us would hide behind the rock or simulate falling off)

Sung: *"Two blind jellyfish, two blind jellyfish, two blind jellyfish sitting on a rock"*

Etc…. Till

Sung: *"No blind jellyfish, no blind jellyfish, no blind jellyfish sitting on a rock"*

Said: *"Then a wave put one back on"* and everyone cheers "Yay!"

Sung: *"One blind jellyfish, one blind jellyfish, one blind jellyfish sitting on a rock"*

so it goes on till they are all back on the rock then ….

A wave comes and washes them all away - "boo hoo"!

We became known as the 3 Blind Jelly fish and even made our own shirts. When Penny left to go to school in the UK, Helen Busbridge took her place.

Amanda, Samara and Penny the original 'Three Blind Jellyfish'

CHAPTER SIX

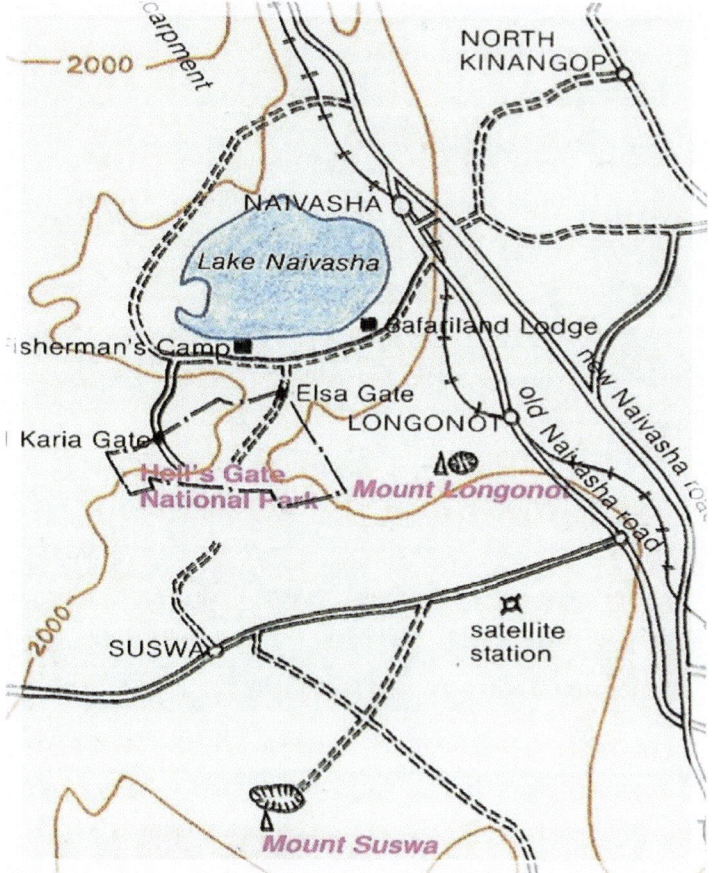

Map 5: Mt Longonot and Hells Gate in relation to Lake Naivasha

Mt Longonot 2777m (9,100 ft)

Mt Longonot & Hells Gate Navigation & Lion

This was a trip to put into practice our navigational skills learned in the classroom and practiced on various preceding expeditions all leading towards the Expedition Award.

Mt Longonot is another caldera that rises about 700m above the Rift Valley floor. There are steam jets that rise from the crater floor which indicate that it is still dormant rather than extinct. It is located about 60 km North West of Nairobi and South of Lake Naivasha.

The first part of this navigation was very straightforward as it was a case of following the main path up to the crater rim and then walking round to the summit. From the summit we headed down in a Westerly direction towards Hells Gate, the end destination being Fishers Tower where we were to meet up with Mr Munro.

From here it became more technical, or 'bundu bashing' a term fondly used when navigating cross country through the African bush and thorny shrubs. The maps we used were poor black and white photocopies which made the whole exercise slightly more challenging, but we managed (see map 6).

Amanda, Penny and I were in one group and our friends Duncan, Heilko and Graham in the other. It is extremely hot and dry and in walking down from the summit towards Buni, a ridge on leg 4, we spotted a little acacia tree with a spot of shade and a rock underneath it so it seemed ideal to get out of the sun. This looked the perfect lunch spot and so we were heading purposefully towards it, chatting merrily about this and that, until we got a bit closer and saw 'the rock' sit up and look at us in a "this is my shade" kind of way! Well, any guesses what it was? Light brown coloured, blending in perfectly with the surrounding murram. Our hearts were racing and we 'calmly' altered our course of direction searching quickly for an alternative spot. This lioness had chosen our spot so it was prudent to leave her to it. Fortunately hunting in the heat of the day isn't what lions tend to do, or maybe she had eaten recently but one of us

would still have made a tasty meal! Suffice to say none of us paused to pull out a camera and take a picture!

We had not gone much further after our near miss with the lion, when we heard thundering hooves and felt the vibrations in the ground coming from behind a small hillock just ahead. Before I knew it Penny and Amanda had scarpered, with me yelling "What's the problem?" and they, shouting back, "Buffalo!" As there was nowhere to run or hide, I had to stand my ground. Actually, it turned out to be a herd of cows belonging to the Maasai, but afterwards we recognised the potential dangers of the wild animals around us.

An experience to share with our grandchildren we all thought once we had safely found our way to Fishers Tower and to all have passed that navigation exercise with the additional tale to tell!

On the way back from this trip I distinctly remember Duncan the driver stopping to buy

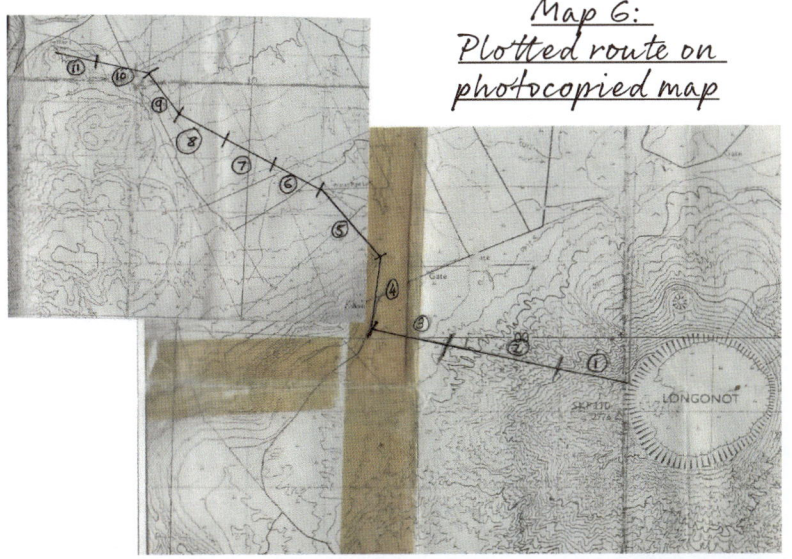

Map 6: Plotted route on photocopied map

Our route card with timings and bearings

rabbits from the side of the road, we suspected for eating rather than as pets but we never questioned it.

Lightweight camping tactics & general anecdotes

Most of our expeditions involved carrying your rucksacks with everything you needed for the trip, mainly because often the bus dropped us at one location and picked us up in another. So, because of that, we became masters of keeping the weight of what we carried to a minimum. Cutting the ends off our toothbrushes and making sure the toothpaste tube only had enough for the trip are examples of shaving off the grams. This was fine until the trip's return was delayed for some reason like getting lost or stuck somewhere, then it became a problem! Another major saving was not taking a tent, OK I hear you ask, where did you sleep? Well, we managed to get hold of 'mortuary bags', yes, exactly that. Big heavy duty black plastic bags which we slept in! On some trips these were perfectly acceptable and we only got a little damp with condensation but it was a different story up Mt Kenya !

At altitude the nights are cold and it was a bit like sleeping in what one can only imagine was a deep freezer. As you rolled over in the night everything crunched and in the morning the condensation on the inside had turned into icicles ! There were a few of our party who decided, probably wisely, to sleep in the mountain hut at that particular campsite, but we considered them to be wimps!

The other big saving in weight was food and a real treat was pot noodles from the UK. Lightweight but a bit on the bulky side but a treat none the less. Another thing Amanda and I would do was to prepare our lunches consisting of two small Barvita biscuits, which are about 8cm long by 4cm wide very thin whole wheat sugar free biscuits with small holes in them. We would put butter on them with marmite and wrap them in cling film, then when we ate them, the marmite and butter would swirl out of the holes!

Early starts were quite common on expeditions, especially when meeting up

Penny, Amanda & Jackie sleeping in mortury bags

MY EARLY LIFE IN KENYA

Amanda 'the hairdresser' using penknife scissors on Samara's hair!

Mt Kenya trips

We made a number of visits up Mt Kenya sometimes with the expedition club and at other times on geography field trips. There are many different routes to explore up the mountain and we did most of them in our time at Hillcrest. Mt Kenya is the highest mountain in Kenya and the second highest in Africa. The main peaks are Batian and Nelion, with the former, being the highest at, an altitude of 5199m/17,057 ft.

There were numerous other peaks around the mountain and the highest non-technical point was Pt Lenana at 4,985 m.

The mountain has its own weather system with amazing flora and fauna that changes as you gain altitude with the dense rainforests and bamboo lower down then up through the mountain moorlands, giant heathers and

with the bus as it was such a hit and miss occurrence. Often a campfire conversation would involve a load of banter from events of the day followed by a brief on our departure the next morning. Our morning muster time was defined by the 'Sparrow tweet' and if it was an early start the phrase would be 'up at Sparrow Fart', which is considerably earlier than Sparrow tweet'! (a term which perhaps would not be used today) I guess you had to be there really to see the joke but it did become part of our expedition vocabulary.

Often once camp was set there was time to kill before the light disappeared and various antics took place depending on the mood. Exploring locally, playing British Bulldogs, moving peoples' tents, messing around in rivers, all lots of fun after a hard day of walking. On another occasion the weather was so foul, wet and rainy we just stayed in our tents and played cards. These were an essential item on a trip or cut hair with penknife scissors as Penny and Amanda decided to do for me on one expedition!

The main peaks
1. Pt Lenana
2. Batian
3. Nelion

then the high-altitude plants such as giant lobelia that have adapted to the high daytime temperatures and the night time freeze. On the lower slopes of the mountain in the forests there were elephant, buffalo and other forest dwellers, higher up you would see hyrax and very occasionally duiker, a very small antelope about the size of a small greyhound, but these were very shy.

The main peaks certainly in the 1980's had permanent glaciers and during the rains sometimes even snow. Hence the early explorers being surprised to see snow on the equator.

Mt Kenya National Park is about a 4-hour drive from Nairobi depending on the route you take and where you are going.

As you can imagine the roads on the mountain were quite treacherous and often

Rock hyrax on Mt Kenya

Common Duiker

impassable during the rains and so sometimes the bus got stuck and ended up walking to our destination.

Our first trip up the mountain was via the Old Moses Route which is north of Naro Moro. I am unsure of the origins of the name but it is the shortest way to the peaks. The bus took us as far as it could but this wasn›t even to the gate at the entrance to the park. This is at an altitude of 2,400m (7,900ft) so it meant we were already starting our walk 2,000 ft higher than our normal altitude in Nairobi which is 5,500ft. The first part of the walk was through bamboo forests and as we gained height the vegetation became moorland, covered with giant heathers which when wet became known as the "vertical bog". The challenge then was to walk on clumps of more

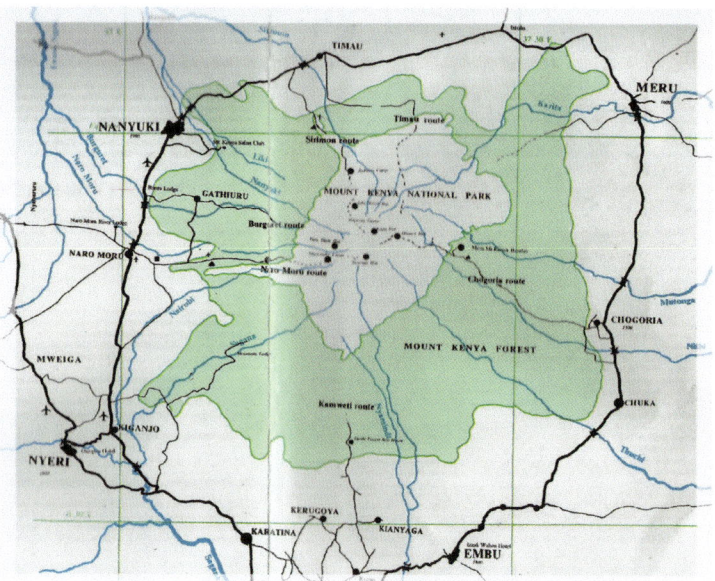

Map 7: Routes up Mt Kenya taken on various trips over the years

solid ground, which if you missed, meant you ended up in a dark wet and very soggy peat bog and invariably wet feet!

On this particular trip up the mountain, we stayed in various mountain huts which were extremely basic, dirty and smelly so often it was more pleasant to set up our own camps nearby.

Walking at altitude is extremely difficult, the lack of oxygen in the air makes everything a real effort no matter how fit and strong you are. Doing anything, even remotely strenuous, is extremely hard and there is an overwhelming urge to stop and rest frequently. Sometimes the altitude brings on a headache so keeping hydrated is very important. One way to progress up the mountain is to think only of getting one foot in front of the other and setting small goals or targets to reach and just keep going till you get there. Natural needs like a 'wee' were satisfied behind bushes etc while on the march!

Basic mountain hut, some slept in it others camped, regardless we always had a campfire to keep us warm & tell stories round.

We were endeavouring to climb to 8,500 ft to get to Point Lenana the third highest peak of the three that constitutes Mt Kenya. At that altitude every step is hard and the going slow.

The mountain lies on the equator and the sun rises at 6.30 every morning and sets at around 6.30 every evening with very little variation during the year. It happens very quickly, almost like the lights going out, unlike the long sunsets you get in the northern hemispheres. The changing colours are, however, something to behold.

Because of the altitude, walking at night when the air is more dense is easier and it is common practice to start the final push to the summit in the early hours of the morning, or the middle of the night. This has the benefit not only of more oxygen in the denser colder air, but the stars are absolutely beautiful, so bright, so clear. It is as though you can reach up and touch them. The clear air, the absence of light means the heavens are aglow. The brightness means that even if there is no moon, you can still walk by their light once your eyes adjust!

The other fascination is that the ground freezes overnight and the moisture in it becomes icicles, pushing up small stones and rocks that lie within and on top of it. If you were to get down to ground level and view it side on, it is like millions of mini ice columns, magical!

We had a 1am start from Austrian Hut at the base of the peaks, one of the many mountain huts, and commenced our trudge up the scree and scramble over the boulders to the summit of Point Lenana. Someone had managed to boil some water and made a brew to warm us a little but we needed to get going. We set off, crunching over the miniature ice columns, using the light from the stars and moon to pick our way up the ridge and the light reflecting off the Lewis glacier from the moon glow also helped. This whole experience is amazing and a roller coaster ride of feelings and emotions and made waking up in the middle of the night when it feels like you have only just got comfortable on the hard cold ground, getting dressed in our sleeping bags worthwhile, a trick we had learned was to keep your clothes in your sleeping bags making getting dressed in the cold morning slightly more pleasant. Not so nice was pushing your feet into your boots which had quite literally frozen overnight and it always seemed to take ages before they thawed and softened!

The final hour before the dawn always feels like the coldest of the night. However, our timing couldn't have been better and as we arrived at the summit as the African dawn was breaking. The sky gradually lit up extinguishing the stars like street lights, at first a silver line in the sky pushed away the dark blue of the night. This quickly warmed to gold before turning fire red casting amazing colours over the main peaks and glacier just before the big bright ball of the sun emerged on the horizon. As the rays caught us, we immediately began to warm up. This is the most amazing and exhilarating sight to behold and many climbers and walkers doubtless have experienced this, but when it's you it feels like you are the first and only one. It is incredibly special.

Going back down, the descent, to the Hut that we left in the early hours is quite a different story. You have daylight, gravity and increasing levels of oxygen making it much easier. You still have to go carefully so as not to twist an ankle and it can be hard on your knees and you get down in a quarter of the time you spent toiling to get up, but it was well worth the hard grind. Four hours of up takes only one hour to come down. Scree running was especially fun, the scree is a mass of loose stones so you just run, jump and slide, only taking care not to get caught on a solid rock.

Later that day it snowed; and as Kenyan kids we hadn't seen much of this white stuff that falls from the sky! So, we just had to climb back up to the Lewis glacier to do a bit of tobogganing down the steeper parts which was great fun.

On this expedition we actually had mountain guides to help us get back down to where the bus was parked which was just as well as I'm not sure we would have made it through the bamboo forest! We arrived at the bus at a very respectable 3.30pm but the bus wouldn't start so the guides headed off down the mountain in search of help, returning sometime later with a land rover which they

Amanda, Samara and Peter Payne on the Lewis glacier below Pt Lenana

managed to obtain. This was then used to tow us in the bus back down the mountain track to Naro Moro town. By the time we got there it was just after midnight with a bus full of very tired and hungry school children. We found an Inn which kindly rustled up a meal of egg, sausages and bread at 1am in the morning, which was very welcome. We then slept in the back of the bus which was parked down some ally and the next morning we drove back to school. Everyone was in school lessons when we got back, tired dirty and dishevelled but we thought it 'cool' but not so sure our parents did! This was my 11th expedition and my diary I noted "THE BEST TRIP SO FAR!"

Our pre-Mt Kilimanjaro acclimatization trip was spent up Mt Kenya with some of the party just walking at altitude and a smaller group of us, who were going to attempt a glacier ascent on Mt Kilimanjaro, practicing with ice axes and crampons on the Joseph Glacier. Crampons are spikes that you strap onto the bottom of your boots which enable you to climb and walk on icy glaciers. We trained to cross crevasses and to enact rescues, although we did have some issues with the crampons staying on our boots, it was fun non the less.

The geography field trip had a number of members who were less experienced so it was our chance to assist in tent pitching and helping them to enjoy the outdoor world. The Chogoria route is one of the most scenic and what a great field trip, glacier lakes, volcanic

CHAPTER SIX

Amanda, Helen and Samara with the Gorges Valley behind us.

Amanda looking back down the Gorges valley with Lake Michaelson below with giant groundsel plants.

plugs, glaciers and measuring the poles on the glacier etc. On this occasion the bus picked us up from the other side of the mountain and amazingly it all went to plan and we managed the now obligatory stop off at the Elephant Inn Castle, for chips and ketchup! I think the bus just heads there on its own!

Whatever the route there were some common themes with our trips and one that became a legend was always to stop at the 'Elephant Inn Castle' in the town of Karatina. It was a town we always seemed to go through but The Elephant Inn Castle did the best chunky chips with tomato ketchup. It was common to stop there on the way up and from memory it was about 3hrs from school and gave us a good and often much needed energy supply for the inevitable pushing of the bus up a muddy track later on in the day. And always if we had time on the way back off the mountain on the way home, we stopped off again.

Ndoto Mountains – otherwise known as "Luggered in the NFD" April 1988

There were many more adventures and another which included an air rescue, was in the Northern Frontier District (NFD). This was a long way north, so far in fact that the tarmac roads ran out and much of the journey up to the Ndotos was on rough, and corrugated murram roads and a two-day drive to get there via Gilgil, Nyahururu, Rumuruti, Maralal and Baragoi. The trip was in the holidays and planned to be back in time for the start of term. Yes, I hear you thinking that wasn't to be …. And indeed, you would be right.

These roads were also full of 'luggas'. A lugga is a dry riverbed prone to flash floods, and it became a running joke to count the number of luggas we drove through and how many we needed to dig or push the bus out from.

When we finally got to where we were going, we found the campsite was on a river which had rocks which were fairly smooth and also a chain of pools. This was just perfect rock sliding territory and we spent many hours sliding down ruining costumes and shorts, but having masses of fun, also we held a 'bum-slide championships' won by Duncan 'snake' Lindsay for the longest slide and Laurence's comment of 'it doesn't hurt coz it's soft rock'.

We had a few days of amazing walks around the hills, swimming in rock pools and exploring the area generally. On the last night we decided to sleep on the rocks, Ian Munro said it won't rain. We hadn't been on the rocks

The bum slides down the river before the flash flood

The river the next morning, no slides to be seen!

Map 8
The route we took to get to the Ndoto Mountains, it took 2 days

long when it did start to rain so we abandoned the rocks and the equipment retreating to our tents which were just up the bank from the river. Four hours and 4 inches of rain later the river had risen by 15 feet, the heaviest rain since 1970! Well, all the cooking equipment, Duncan's 'my Mum's going to kill me' hi-tech trainers, Mr Payne's book including the beer and many other items were now being washed down the river heading towards the coast.

CHAPTER SIX

The morning found us cup less, cutlery less and beer-less!

After breakfast out of bowls made out of UHT milk packets, we set off in the bus. That day we covered the amazing distance of 2 km! Mainly by pushing and digging. Mr Munro disappeared in search of something for supper, he returned with 3 chickens which must have been marathon runners and they were fairly rubbery by the time they were cooked!

The American missionaries stationed at Ngurunit kindly invited us to go to supper one night and stay in their guest house which had a video and water bed – luxury. The roads were flooded so getting out of the area was a real challenge and parts of the murram roads had been washed away in the flash floods. The next day we loaded the bus with rocks and branches to build the road up so we could start making our way home. Due to some security issue in Kenya at the time we couldn't use the missionaries' radios to alert parents in Nairobi that we would be delayed on our return because the roads had been washed away. We weren't late yet but there was no way we would be back on schedule with only travelling between 2 & 5 km a day with the total distance being about 450km!

We pushed on undeterred, needing to purchase the odd goat as rations to keep us all fed. The details of this are not for the faint hearted but essentially a live goat was bought from local people, which was then passed to the driver to kill, skin and prepare

The bus stuck in a lugga again!

Pushing the bus through the Milgis Poi in the background

for roasting. In Kenya roast goat or meat is generally cooked over an open fire is called 'nyama choma', cooked/burnt meat.

Progress was slow until we reached the Milgis river which had burst its banks and then more rain fell making it even harder to move. We had to retreat to Ngurunit. By now we were late and unknown to us an aerial search party had been deployed. My Dad had asked Jens Hessel who owned a Cessna 206, a 6-seater, to assist. At least with this plane there was an ability to retrieve a few of us at a time. They spotted our stuck bus and landed on a dry bit of road and proceeded to ferry us out and eventually back to Nairobi. Mwangi the driver was left with the bus until a bus

Ian Munro, Masaai, Jens Hessel, Samara, Ben Clay, Helen Busbridge and Phil Lewis under the wing of the Cessna 206.

Jens having landed on the road to pick us up, Ian Munro talking to Dad and Masaai onlookers.

recovery party could be dispatched but there was little point in this until the flood waters had subsided.

Mt Kilimanjaro – December 1987 – 21 to the Top

Mt Kilimanjaro is the highest mountain in Africa with the summit Kibo at 5,895m/19,341 ft. It is believed Kenya gave Mt Kilimanjaro to Tanzania in years gone by hence the kink in the border between Kenya and Tanzania. Climbing Mt Kilimanjaro can be done entirely by walking but the biggest challenge is the threat of altitude sickness caused by gaining height too quickly. The best way to acclimatise is to spend time at altitude allowing your body to adapt.

This was certainly an expedition not to be missed. The preparation for the trip was very involved, not only the fitness side, but also the logistics of food, porters and transport as there were 21 of us taking part. With the altitude involved this was a serious expedition and the lead up to it involved numerous walks across the Ngong Hills carrying rucksacks to get used to carrying the weight. We also had an acclimatization expedition up Mt Kenya a few days prior to the Kilimanjaro expedition as this would get us up to about 16,000 ft and our bodies would be in a better situation to

Map 9: Mt Kilimanjaro Routes
The Green route was our long haul up Mt Kilimanjaro, the orange route was our descent.

cope with the lack of oxygen in the air.

My Dad was part of the expedition team, to make a cine film of the trip. He had done one previously for a different school up Mt Kenya which was a huge success. This is indeed a fabulous record of the trip; the film was named "21 to the Top".

Mum was instrumental in helping Mr Munro design the menu for the trip and took the lead in purchasing goods and making the meals. Everything was carefully packaged up for each day as nutrition on such a trip was essential to achieve success.

Departure day was a 7am start from school so the bus had been loaded the night before. The route we were taking was a long slow ascent up the Shira plateau so about 8 days to ascend the mountain and then two days to come down what is best known as the 'tourist route' ie shortest route up, but often not successful as altitude sickness is a total show stopper.

We arrived at the Shira Park gate in the early evening and were left setting up camp and feeding ourselves while Ian and Sammy went to fetch our porters. It was a requirement of the Park and also a necessity to have porters assist in carrying food and equipment. This provided employment for locals but also reduced the load each of us were to carry. The age range of students were 14 – 18-year-olds.

The next day we packed up camp, eager and

ready to go but still waiting for Ian and Sammy to return with the porters. The day was spent playing cards, rounders and keeping ourselves occupied. They got back with the bus load of porters at 4pm when it started to rain so camp was re-pitched with the start delayed by a day or to when there was a break in the weather. Ian sorted out the porters loads which involved weighing the rucksacks as they were paid per day and weight carried so everything had to carefully recorded.

We started the next day very excited about the challenge ahead. It was a fairly gentle 4-hour walk, gradually ascending through the giant heathers with occasional and daunting glimpses of the glaciated south western face before us and reaching our campsite for the night. This gave us a great opportunity to pose for photos with our final destination looking some way off.

The next few days consisted of steady walking and a gradual ascent of the mountain. The trick was not to gain too much altitude in one day so sometimes the day was short but then the time spent in the new campsite would be part of the acclimatisation process. To fill in the time we set up camp and then explored around the area with a lighter load, often clearing up rubbish left by other mountain tourists.

As the days went by, various members of the expedition team began to suffer the effects of the altitude but again with the slow ascent this subsided. There weren't many that didn't feel it one way or another.

A small group of us; including Amanda, Ian Munro and I were due to attempt a route up the Heim glacier to the crater rim, so hence our training on the Mt Kenya trips. However, at one of our camps we met 2 men of the British Army who had had to retreat off the glacier as it was too dangerous. One camp later when we could actually see the glacier, we realised this was not to be attempted. A decision was made therefore for the 'glacier group' to go on ahead of the main party and do the final ascent a day ahead of the others and spend a night in the main crater floor.

Barafu Hut, at 4,600m, was the base for the final summit push. At this altitude there is no vegetation and just a lot of rock. After a supper of tinned mackerel and mash we got our heads down, sleeping in the hut as we were carrying our tents up to the rim for our night in the crater. It was an extremely early start, waking at 1am packing up our sleeping bags, wrapping up warm and starting the long slow slog up the scree slopes. There were a number of reasons for the early start. At that time the scree slope is mainly frozen so less sliding back down and the other more important reason was as the air is cooler it is denser and so more oxygen in the air. Once the sun comes up it gets extremely hot and even more difficult to breath. It is almost impossible to describe the sensation of not having enough oxygen to do anything. We kept close together and quickly fell into a steady rhythm, stopping every half

CHAPTER SIX

an hour for a drink and rest. The stops weren't too long as it was so cold.

There was an impressive sunrise as we were above the clouds, but the as dawn broke and we were higher, everything got harder. I'm not sure being able to see where you were going actually helped!

Arriving at the crater rim was cause for a big celebration but we still needed to walk round to the summit. We left our rucksacks and walked on round to the summit which I have to say is not the most inspiring but what an amazing feeling of being quite literally on the roof of Africa. Quite a moment, and to be there with my Dad was very emotional.

We camped that night in the crater at 18,700ft which was extremely uncomfortable but exhilaration the next morning when we saw the main party arrive at the crater rim which made it worthwhile. We packed up and climbed out of the crater for a team photo of all 21 of us at the top.

Samara and David Lowe on the Roof of Africa Kibo 5,895m/19,341ft

The whole party then descended to Barfu hut, collected our belongs and began our elated descent down the mountain. What took 8 days to come up only took 2 days to get down and although going down was hard on the legs, our lungs were loving all the extra oxygen that each step brought. It was such fun and we even had a hail storm but that didn't matter much. Our spirits were very high and nothing seemed to matter. Once in the rainforest section we stopped by a stream and this seemed an ideal opportunity to dunk everyone into it. I don't think anyone escaped and some took the humour better than others!

Summit push 1am start up the scree

"21 at the Top" – the full group on the crater rim

We finished our trip with a night in the relative luxury of the Kibo hotel and a dinner in the restaurant before heading back to Nairobi on time and on the right day. Quite a feat! So, an enormous success with all twenty-one reaching the top, thanks to Mum and her team of helpers and of course to the superb organisation of our "dedicated leader" Ian Munro.

Closing notes on the Expedition section

Looking back and reflecting on the various expeditions I went on, I was fortunate to see wonderful sites and enjoy the company of others, many of whom are still my friends today.

I also learnt some essential truths about life which have stayed with me, such as, through teamwork almost anything can be achieved and loyalty is all to your friends and is paramount. Character building is an old cliché but to overcome adversity in difficult conditions does indeed build confidence in your ability to look problems in the eye and overcome them.

To the people who arranged these adventures and took care of us, together with the Parents who supported and encouraged us, I dedicate this chapter.

CHAPTER SIX

List of Expeditions Logged by Samara

1	Mt Suswa Caving & Orienteering	13/14 Sept 1985
2	Mt Suswa Day trip caving	22 Sept 1985
3	Lost in the Loitas	27–30 Sept 1985
4	Aberdare Mountains	11–14 Oct 1985
5	Lukenya Climbing	9–10 Nov 1985
6	Tsavo Climbing	29 Nov – 1 Dec 1985
7	Lukenya Climbing	18–19 Jan 1986
8	Chyulu Hills	22–24 Feb 1986
9	Longonot/Hells Gate Navigation Exercise	8–9 Mar 1986
10	Nguruman Mountains	1–4 May 1986
11	Mt Kenya – Old Moses Route	30 May – 3 Jun 1986
12	Lukenya Climbing	27–28 Sept 1986
13	Ndoto Mountains	9–15 Dec 1986
14	Mt Kenya – Icy Mike trip	30 Jan – 1 Feb 1987
15	Lukenya Climbing	22 Mar 1987
16	Mt Suswa Caving	9–10 May 1987
17	Maparasha Hills	12–13 Jun 1987
18	Nguruman Hills	7–9 Jul 1987
19	Mt Kenya – Siromen Route	4–7 Dec 1987
20	Mt Kilimanjaro – 21 to the top	11–20 Dec 1987
21	Mt Kenya – Chogoria Route Geography trip	11–15 Feb 1988
22	Ndoto Mountains – Luggered in the NFD	18–28 Apr 1988
23	Lukenya Climbing	26 Nov 1988
24	Mt Meru – Tanzania	2–5 Dec 1988

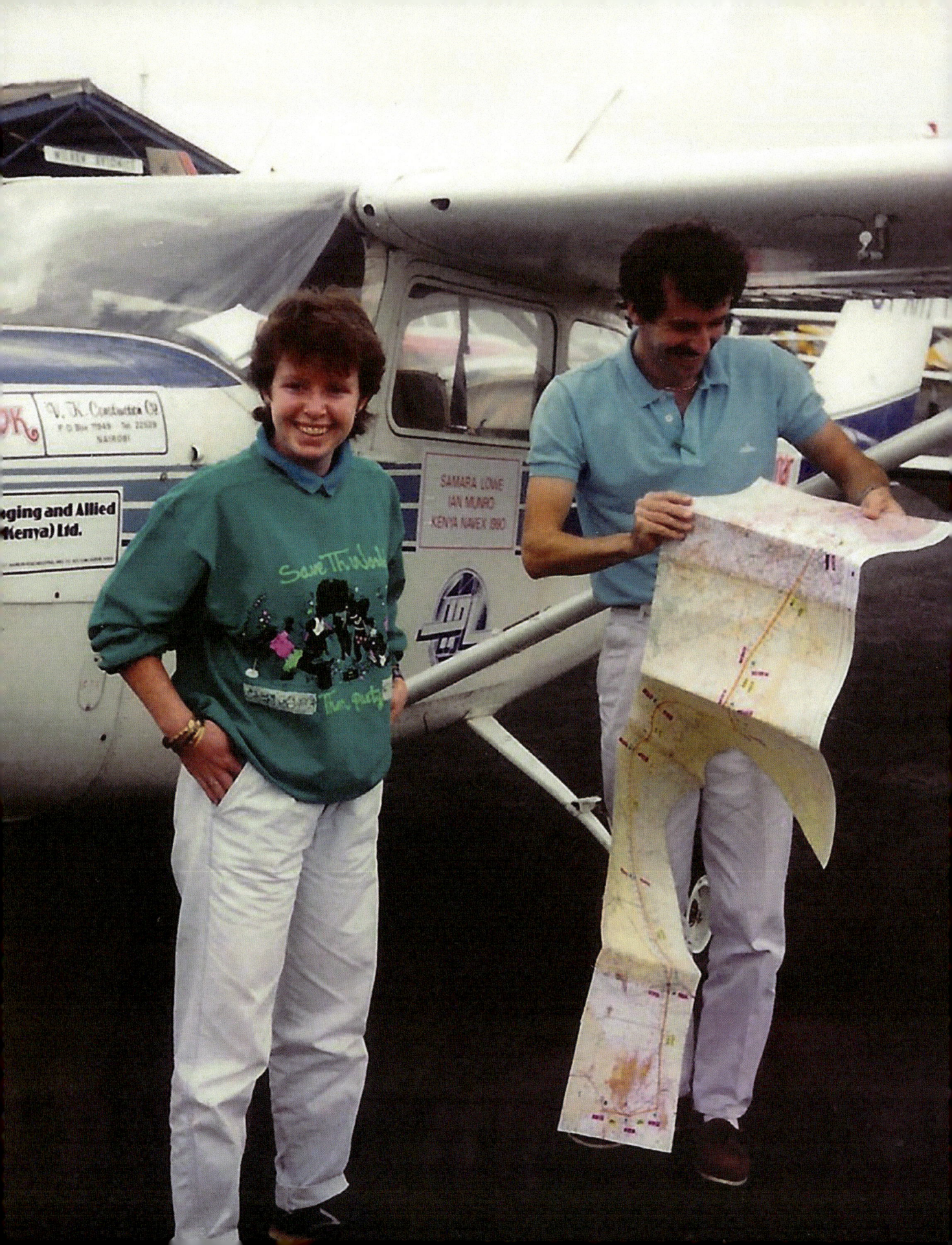

Chapter Seven
FLYING
(September 1979 – December 1984)

Learning to fly

1989: The seed is sown for the next phase of my life

Navex Competitions

Flying Experiences 'Business pilot under supervision'

CHAPTER SEVEN

Learning to Fly 28 Aug 1988 – 24 May 1989

WHILST FLYING HAS GIVEN me great pleasure over the years, it also provided the first great loss of my life, my Father.

However, it all began on Sunday 28th August, the day before my 17th Birthday, when Dad asked me if I would like to learn to fly? Well, the answer was a most definite yes please! Dad was the Chief Flying instructor at Pegasus Flyers, a flying training school attached to the Aero Club of East Africa at Wilson Airport. We went down to Wilson to start on the first lesson. As Dad had lots of other students at weekends, I settled into a few books about learning to fly and the new set of skills I would need for this adventure I had embarked on.

The training aircraft we flew were Cessna 150 Aerobats which are little 2-seater high wing planes. I remember the first thing I had to do was to learn to walk around the aeroplane and carry out checks which are a combination of both visual and physical to make sure nothing obvious was amiss and to check the fuel and oil status. Once in the plane, there were the internal and cockpit checks as well as checking the instrumentation, which you can follow on a check list specific to the type of aircraft. The captain of an aeroplane sits in the left-hand seat, so as a student pilot this is where you sit and your instructor sits beside you. The controls are dual so it can be controlled from either side. The difference being the main instruments needed are positioned in favour of the left-hand seat.

Next, was starting up. Another checklist and then learning how to taxi out and manoeuvre the plane remembering you have long wings so the spaces you fit though need to be considered. Once we were airborne you spend your time getting used to the environment of the cockpit, how to hold the control column and what you expect to see out of the window. One of the most important lessons early on is the transfer of control of the plane from instructor to student and importantly looking out and being aware of your surroundings. The first flight lasted 40 minutes, which quite literally flew by, and I loved every moment of it, I was so grateful to Dad for the opportunity.

The next day was my birthday and my presents were mainly things that I would

The Pegasus Flyers hangar and 5Y-AZW the Cessna 150 Aerobat that I did most of my flying training in.

need for flying. Log book, knee pad, flight computer, flight protractor and ruler. The day was spent having a photo taken and collecting the forms for my Student Pilot's licence so now I was all set to start on my flying adventure.

From early September I flew most Saturdays and Sundays but it was the case of fitting lessons in around my riding commitments as well as Jackie and David's activities. Gradually I worked my way through the flying training syllabus. Effects of controls, taxiing, flying straight and level, turns, climbing and descending, stalls and spin recovery. Yes, for anyone that flies now, in those days we did learn how to recover from a spin. Alongside all the aerial training there was quite a lot to learn on the theory side. This is known as ground school. Logically if you understand what the forces are that effect the flight surfaces and the way an aeroplane will react when put into various configurations, it made the flying exercise in the air bit easier.

Handling the plane up in the air soon became more natural and good skills and habits were formed. Also using the radio to talk to the airfield control tower began and then the circuit work.

Flying a circuit involves taking off and flying a rectangular pattern based on the runway as you can see from the diagram. You take off, climb out, turn once you reach a certain height, turn again to fly

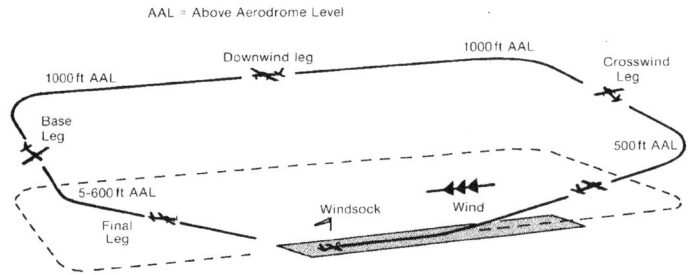

Fig.12-5. The Normal Circuit Pattern is Flown at 1000 ft AAL.

down parallel to the runway. This is the downwind leg, then at the appropriate point turn back towards the runway, start your descent and turn onto the final approach to land. Each stage you learn is very much reliant on various key points in the pattern that you become familiar with at the airfield you are flying from. These are the various landmarks or positions relative to the runway. The tricky bit of course is getting the plane safely back on the ground, which is a fine judgement, but there are a number of factors that can help with getting it right. The wind direction and speed, your approach speed, the power you have on and a few more technical considerations.

When you are learning and doing circuit work you will do 'touch and go' circuits which means you come in land and then take off again allowing for quite a few more practice landings in your flight time.

It is also important to learn from an early stage what to do if things go wrong such as an engine failure after take-off. You are taught how to react, what actions to take and not to panic in the unlikely event that this situation

CHAPTER SEVEN

should arise. This is all in preparation for your 'First Solo' a milestone in every pilot's flying journey. Your instructor has to get you trained to a point where he or she is confident you can take off safely, fly a circuit and land back completely on your own.

Of course, as a student you know when you are approaching your first solo flight as a lot of time is spent in the circuit. I knew I was getting close; I had flown over the weekend and I knew that my landings were consistently improving. I had another flight booked after school on the Monday 7th November 1988 in the Cessna 150 with the registration 5Y-AZW, I finished my maths mock exam and then Mum took me down to Wilson and there we met Dad. He and I flew one circuit and were cleared for a 'touch and go' but after I landed Dad took control by saying "I have control".

I knew this was it, as he contacted the tower

Wilson airport from the air the runway you can see running, Nairobi city centre in the background and Nairobi National Park below. (photo NOT taken on my 1st Solo!)

and requested the first exit and clearance to hold on the taxiway as the student was to be going First Solo – WOW, my heart raced, my legs felt like jelly, Dad brought the plane to a standstill with the engine still running. He briefed me as he was getting out and I was to do exactly what we had been doing. Do my pre-take-off checks, get my clearance as normal, take off do one circuit, land and taxi back to the Aero Club. He opened the door got out and secured the harnesses, shut the door then moved back gave me thumbs up and a wave!

Wow again, this is it! Now it was time to concentrate, remember to do what I had been trained to do. Well, what a feeling that was, having done my power and pre-take off checks and got my clearance, I sat at the end of the runway, applied full power and started to roll down the runway. I got airborne a lot quicker than I had before, I guess because there was one less person in the plane. Once I was established in the climb and settled on the downwind leg heading towards the Ngong Hills I yelled out with joy "woohoo", it was amazing. I'm not quite sure how to describe this feeling of freedom and elation, looking down at the Nairobi National Park below, Wilson Airport off to the right and the empty seat beside me thinking how great this was. OK time to focus now and get myself down! So, I followed the routine, did the checks, turned onto base leg then the final approach, made my radio calls and came in

Looking towards the Ngong Hills from the 'downwind leg'

and landed. Once I was down, I could see Dad there watching with the most enormous grin on his face. I shut down the plane and got out shaking with excitement, I had done it!

The first solo whilst important, is just part of the training although a significant milestone. There is quite a lot of consolidation and still a massive amount of learning still to be done, and on many of the flights that followed, you would do a few circuits with the instructor first before being let out on your own again. You are very much in that danger zone of having enough experience to get yourself into trouble but not quite enough experience to get yourself out of trouble. Every single flight is unique as conditions vary. Wind, thermals, other air traffic distractions, the radio and sun in your eyes etc and there were a few moments when I found myself rounding out into level flight a bit too high above the runway and thinking the sink would never end before 'arriving' on the tarmac with a bit more of a positive bump than maybe I should and then of course a bounce! Fortunately training aircraft are specifically built to take a bit of hammering as students learn how to land smoothly.

The training continued with lots more landings in different conditions. For example, crosswinds and the aircraft in different configurations, like no flaps, high approaches etc. Then back out into the local area to learn more upper air work steep turns and learning to navigate. The ground school continued weekly alongside the flying, lessons which included all the theory of what we were doing as well as all the rules of the air, weather, navigation etc. all essential before you can get your private pilot's licence as you need to pass all these exams as well. Ground school was an evening at Pegasus with Sir Henry White. Sir Henry was an ex-RAF and Bomber Command pilot, and was one of the few who survived innumerable wartime sorties. A great character and a founder of Pegaus Flyers. Amanda had also started learning to fly so at least we could do ground school together and were often down at the airfield at the same time as the lift sharing helped our Mum's get everyone to where they needed to be.

As part of the licence, you needed to fly a cross country flight so we trained for this by doing various triangular routes. First of all, with Dad to learn the air navigation, plotting and planning the route and flight times. Also, making allowances for any

CHAPTER SEVEN

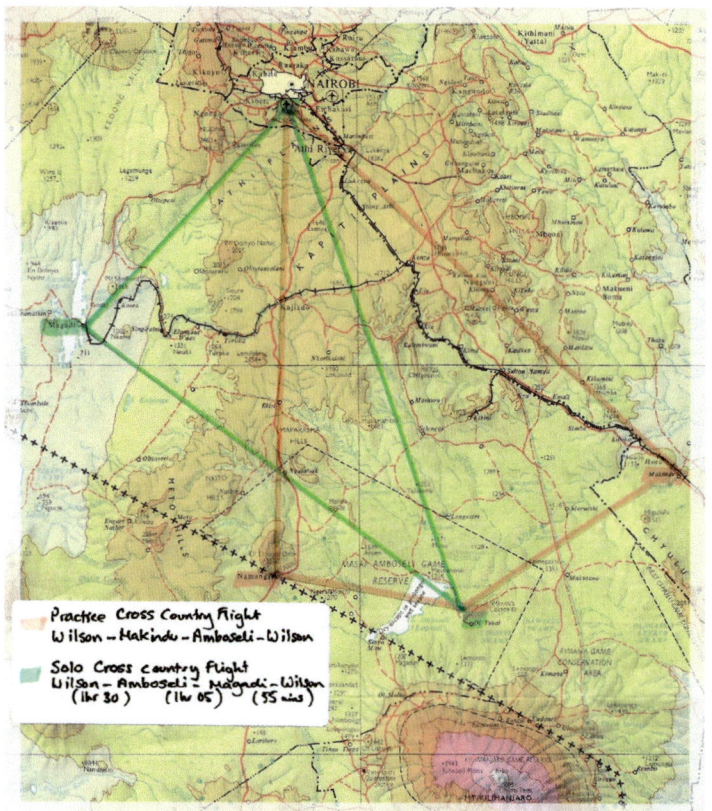

Duel and Solo Cross country flight routes flown.

altitude and various local obstacles. For our land away practice on the 26th March 1989 Dad and I flew from Wilson airport to Makindu (1hr 40min) then on to Amboseli National Park (40mins) then to Namanga (30 mins) near the Kenya/Tanzania boarder and finally returning to Wilson (1 hr 10mins). I remember we took with us water, a flask of coffee and some sandwiches to keep us refuelled and hydrated. I was then set to do my solo cross country the next day. My route from Wilson airport was a 90-minute flight south east to Kilimanjaro Buffalo, a landing strip near one of the lodges in Amboseli National Park. I landed and had to have my paper stamped to prove my arrival, a quick drink then off on my next leg heading north west to Lake Magadi a flight lasting 1hr 5 mins. I landed there and had a slightly longer break, something to eat and drink under the wing of the plane. Lake Magadi is a soda lake and exceedingly hot, so once refreshed and my maps had been rearranged, I set off on the final leg back to Wilson a flight lasting 55mins.

crosswinds you encountered and adjusting the headings accordingly. Also being aware of key navigational features to pinpoint your location etc and once I could demonstrate a good understanding, I was sent off to do a solo route. I did the reverse of the one I had done with Dad so the turning points were at least familiar but it nevertheless still looks different flying in the other direction.

For your licence you need to actually land away at different airstrips which again gives you experience of different things to look out for. Landing somewhere unfamiliar, included considerations of airstrip length,

Lake Magadi – a saline, alkaline lake recharged by saline hot springs, fast evaporation leaves a pink soda crust which is mined.

Samara's logbook entry "PPL test passed"

It was fantastic to be flying this route alone and although I knew the ground below from some of the school and family trips it does look very different from the air. At least there were big land marks along the way. I got back safely and once again was exhilarated by this achievement and delighted to have completed that phase of the training. It was now time to consolidate, go back and refresh on all the air work, emergencies, different landings and circuits to prepare for my test flight with an examiner to get my licence.

I had my test with Mr N.B Patel, he was an examiner and a Kenya Airways Captain and as with all flight tests there are certain areas that need to be addressed so they are satisfied you can deal with emergencies and are safe in the air.

The flight profile, or planned execution, is briefed before we get anywhere near the plane. This is so you have an idea of what is coming, so no surprises except when he might pull a simulated engine failure on you and check you take the appropriate course of action. My test was done during the week so I had to be collected a bit early from school to get to the airfield in time.

The flight went as briefed and I remember that it seemed to have gone well, I didn't really know how I had done until Mr Patel handed me my log book which now had 'PPL TEST PASSED' written in it. Wow, wow hurray 24 May 1989 and I had my private pilot's licence. The funny thing was in Kenya you couldn't learn to drive until you were 18 years old, so I was in this peculiar situation where Mum needed to accompany me driving on my 'L' plates down to Wilson airport so I could go flying! Surreal!

1989 – The seeds are sown for the next phase of my life

This was another busy year with A levels in November and by now, I had started to think about careers and where to go with my life. I always thought having a plan was a good idea, and as opportunities arise a different direction may be taken. I had thought about becoming an Air Traffic Controller as being an airline pilot just didn't excite me. However, soon after my flying training began the Royal Air Force began to accept female pilots, so flying rather than sitting in a tower sounded a much better option. The Air and Naval attaché in Nairobi, Wing Commander Raley, suggested on our next UK trip to book into RAF Biggin Hill to do what is called a Test in Advance, a 2-day assessment with aptitude tests, interviews and a medical to confirm I was potentially a suitable pilot candidate and maybe avoid disappointment later. We arranged this on our next trip to the UK and was extremely pleased to pass, the only requirement, due to my residency in Kenya, was to spend a year at university before applying for a Pilots Scholarship; Now my goal was to get the A levels I needed and a place at a university that had a University Air Squadron.

From this point I became ever more involved in the world of flying, which was my Father's passion, and very quickly I found myself involved on the Nairobi Airshow organising committee and taking part in anything that involved flying. I started getting checked out on other aircraft and then taking friends flying, my first passenger being Mum, followed by any friends and even teachers. Basically, anyone who wanted to go up! It was great fun.

Ian Munro had also been taught to fly by my Dad and had passed his PPL just 9 months ahead of me and when Ian wasn't doing Motor rallies or partaking in school expeditions, he was flying. Therefore, there were a few opportunities for Ian and I to team up and take part in some air navigational competitions before I went to university.

Navex Competitions

A Navex is a navigational exercise and flying competition where the entrants declare at what speed they will fly their aeroplane for the duration of the route. Speeds of course differ greatly from one aircraft type to another, so the organisers set a navigational course, with turning points and each aircraft is given their start time based on the airspeed they declare. Anticipated arrival times at each turning point are calculated by the organisers. The course to be flown is the same for all aircraft, it just takes longer for those flying at slower speeds. Ground marshals sitting at each turning point record the aircraft registration and the time each plane arrived and turned. As they will have had an expected time of arrival, they would know how many seconds the plane is early or late. They were also to report back if the aircraft is off track or didn't show thus receiving penalty points.

We took part in a few of these Navex rallies, which were in different locations around Kenya but there's no need to describe them all. I have essentially outlined our first experience and one I made the most notes of in my diary and hopefully you will gain an idea of what is involved and the fun we had. This navex was a 1-day participation but later on, rallies ran over 3 days with night stops and so were much more involved. We progressed onto flying the Cessna 172, Reims Rocket, slightly bigger and slightly faster but able to hold our night bags. We even got sponsorship to help with the costs.

As you will have gathered, the object is to declare a speed you know your plane can achieve and a time in which you can complete the course, also to have enough fuel for the journey and to be accurate on your flying. The fastest planes start first and slowest last.

On the Friday, Ian and I headed down to Wilson Airport to get in a practice flight in preparation for our participation in the Rally. There was chaos, because of all the visiting planes from Zimbabwe and elsewhere had arrived. We had to queue for fuel at the pumps, much like a petrol station but for aircraft, and it takes twice as long as there are fuel tanks in both wings and both needed to be filled. Having picked two points to fly between, at different speeds, we worked out our timings and declared a speed that would work for us over the course.

On Saturday morning there was a briefing for all participants at 9am, when we were all given maps and the route which had 17 turning points all of which were given in 6 figure reference points. The rest of the day was spent plotting the points on our maps and working out our precise timings and headings. We plotted our route, taped our maps together and then went home for a good night's sleep to be ready for the next day.

Sunday, we awoke early making sure we had coffee, food and all our maps. Then we had breakfast and were out of the house by 7am. As Ian and I were in the slowest plane we were last to depart meaning extra coffee and

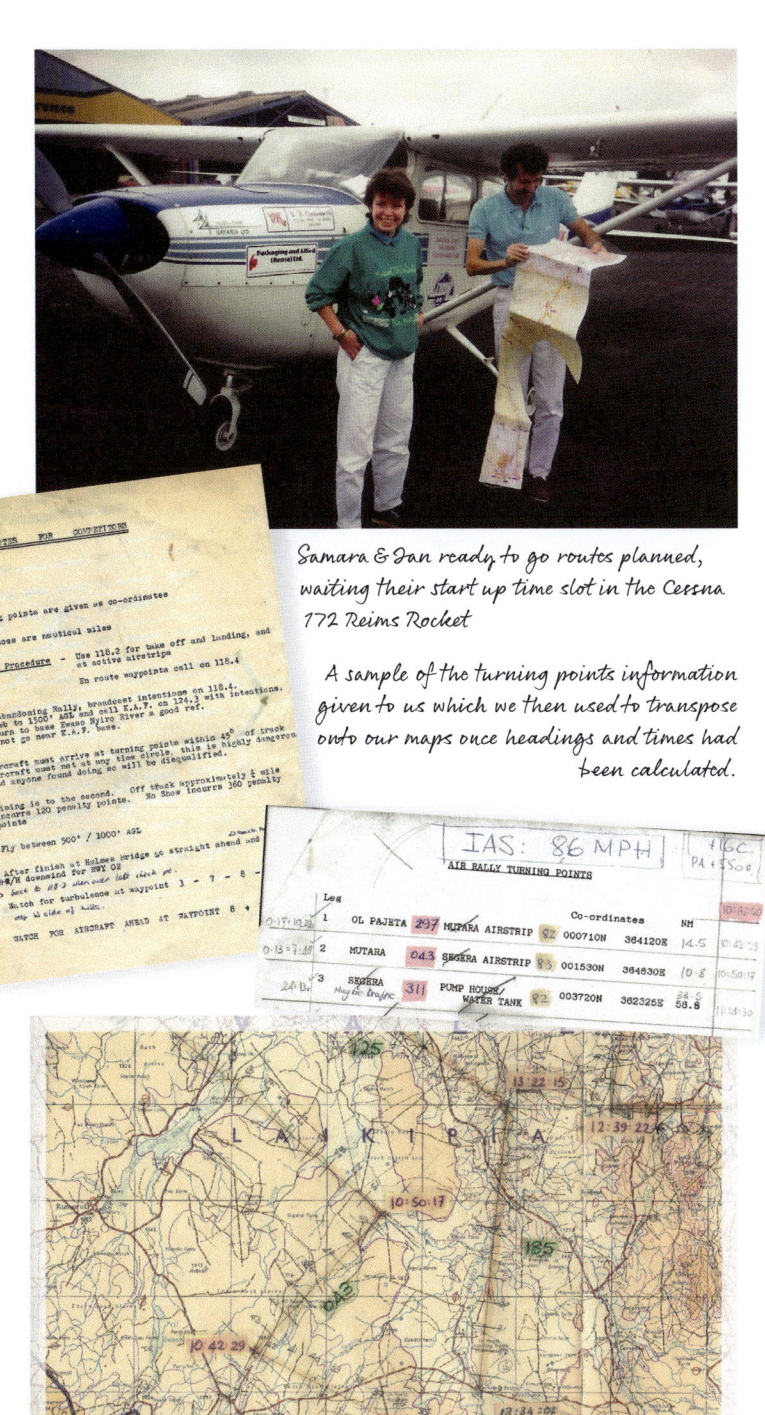

Samara & Ian ready to go routes planned, waiting their start up time slot in the Cessna 172 Reims Rocket

A sample of the turning points information given to us which we then used to transpose onto our maps once headings and times had been calculated.

Level of detail on the route maps with arrival times on turning points to the second.

CHAPTER SEVEN

Jenny Boutwood, Amanda's Mum manning & recording aircraft at one of the turning points somewhere near Lake Magadi

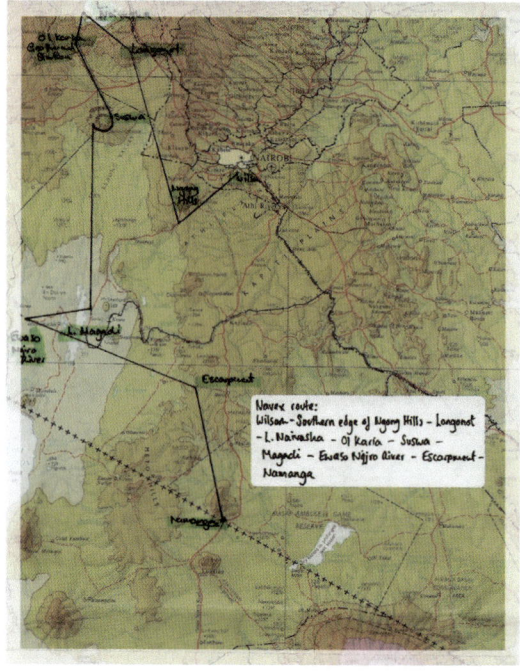

a longer time at breakfast in the Aero Club restaurant. The start was delayed an hour due to the weather and eventually the first of the 38 planes taking part took off at 11am. As we were last and had plenty of time we were interviewed and photographed! Fame of sorts!

Kenya is a beautiful country and so the organisers chose a route that would show it at its best to the many visiting pilots. The course selected (see map) took us over some of Kenya's most iconic landscapes including Lake Magadi.

Ian did the navigating and I flew the plane which worked very well. From what I heard afterwards from people at the check points, we were doing quite well until check point no 22 where we had a 'no show' declared against us, so incurred a 360-point penalty, otherwise we would have been in the top10! Ian flew back to Wilson from Namanga and I did the navigation. We came 17th overall at the end of the day and 4th in the Kenya Navex. Not bad for two rookie pilots and lots of fun too.

Flying Experiences 'Business pilot under supervision'

With Dad's connections on the airfield, his work and his volunteering with the Kenya Wildlife Service (KWS) there were plenty of opportunities to fly some more unusual flights as well as the standard ones. But the bottom line was if it could be done by flying and I could go I was there.

I started to learn aerobatics and as Dad was an aerobatic instructor doing loops,

112

The Ngong Hills from the Rift Valley side

Another trip with a less favourable outcome a report of an elephant carcass, tusks remining. Joyce Poole logging the find.

barrel rolls and stall turns didn't worry me. It was fun and it also taught you more about being able to push the plane to its limits. We did our aerobatic flights over the rift valley using landmarks like the Ngong hills or Mt Suswa as our reference points.

Throughout the year Dad and I did Certificate of Airworthiness test flights on various aircraft as well as engine run ins. Some flights involved pushing the plane to its manufacturer's limits.

A useful skill that Dad taught me was instrument appreciation. This is what to do if one of your flight instruments in the cockpit fails and your need to use the others to help you fly safely which is essential should you inadvertently get into cloud. It is only when you can't see out the window and don't have visual references do you realise just how quickly you can get disorientated.

Another time, Dad was asked to help out by flying vets up to a farm in Laikipia to

Elephants spotted for darting.

dart & tag an elephant so it could be tracked and monitored by elephant researcher Joyce Poole. Sometimes however, what we found was very upsetting as poaching was a huge and very real problem.

In my final few days in Kenya before starting university there was an Airshow where I took part in aerobatics with Dad as well as formation flypasts and assisting in the general running of the day.

Well, what an amazing gap year which afforded me some wonderful times and opportunities.

Chapter Eight

ADVENTURES IN MY GAP YEAR

(December 1989 - October 1990)

Collecting Jackie's A Level results

Secretarial training & general experience gathering

Lawrence safari in the Mara

Flying Jackie & I to a 21st Party

Helping out on school expeditions

Ewaso Nyiro and the 'Safari Surgeons'

Closing lines

CHAPTER EIGHT

Collecting Jackie's A Level results!

I WAS BACK IN KENYA when Jackie was due to get her A level results. The evening before the results were due to be announced many youngsters went out to "Bubbles" a night club in Nairobi. I was the designated driver and during the evening I got chatting to a nice young man who happened to be staying at the headmaster's house. He told me that all the results were laid out on the dining room table and it would be easy to find Jackie's. So, I offered him a lift home and we decided to take a sneaky peak! However, we failed to notice that it had got quite late and Dad was concerned, so he came to check all was OK. He passed us on the Ngong Road and recognising the headlights of the car, he returned home expecting to find us there. As a result, when we finally turned up, he was fuming and wanted to know where we had been! However, we were SO excited with Jackie's results we just had to share our secret. A, A & a B were her grades but Dad had to be cross about something so demanded what was the B. It was in fact Art which was surprising as Jackie is such an amazing artist. However, we could see he was really pleased and so we kept our diversion a secret.

Secretarial Training & experience gathering

Between finishing my A levels in Dec 1989 and starting University in October 1990 I spent most of my time carrying on with my adventures but without the diversion of school. By now, I had my driving licence, which was a great help, and I was in a position to start giving back to the world some of that which I had taken. This included being an assistant on school expeditions, teaching young children to ride, running errands for Mum and Dad, collecting horse food and bulk shopping and much more. I also attended a secretarial course. I persevered with the touch typing but gave up on the short hand, although in hindsight I should have stayed with it as it would have been extremely useful going forward in life. Additionally, I had the most fantastic opportunity to build up my flying experience so I began flying Dad on his work trips.

I was also able to do lots of riding and played social hockey at the local sports clubs, which is much easier to do when you can drive yourself around to the places involved.

Helping on a Lawrence Luxury Safari to the Mara 5 -11th January 1990

During my time between A levels and starting university there was an ideal period to gain some different experience and being in Kenya there was plenty of opportunity for this. David, my younger brother, was very good friends with Guy Lawrence, whose parents, Mike and Heather Lawrence, ran luxury camping safaris around Kenya and an opportunity arose to go and help on one of these. I was paid for my work but actually it was the chance to experience how a luxury safari runs as well as helping friends, that drew me to this.

To prepare, I had met with Heather Lawrence at her house a few days earlier to sort out what I would be expected to do whilst out on Safari with Mike and his clients.

It was 4.30 am on the day I started that the alarm went off and as I had spent the evening packing and hadn't got to bed until 12.30am meant I only had 4 hours sleep. Also, the car that was meant to pick me up at 5am didn't arrive till 5.30am.

We went to Naivasha which is a town in the Rift Valley, by Lake Naivasha, which is where I met Mike Lawrence and his gang. We repacked the Land Cruisers and set off by 8.45am. The clients were from Bermuda and all very nice people and were looking forward to their safari.

The road wasn't very good and the journey was long, but at least it wasn't dusty or desperately muddy and so with various stops etc on the way we arrived at 4pm. The camp was situated in some trees and faced into a clearing which was quite close to the river.

For my part it was mostly confined to making sure that meals were on time and well prepared, that the camp was cleaned and everything was as it should be. However,

The campsite was set up somewhere near this river – the Mara River

for the curious, the toilet facilities were still rather basic, as the campsite was not a permanently established site, and it consisted essentially of a 'long drop' a hole in the ground with a wooden seat over the top and a tent placed around that for privacy. Dear readers, this remember was Africa in the late 1980s.

I went on some of the game drives with the guests and thoroughly enjoyed myself and despite the fact it was hard work, it was very rewarding and I got paid for it.

Hartebeest & zebra in the Mara

A cheetah with her 5 large cubs

However, one incident I remember well was that I was asked to prepare a cake for one of the young guests who had a birthday. I solicited the help of Opongo, the camp Chef to assist.

For a start there was no oven to speak of, nor mixers or any of the modern utensils we take for granted. The starting point was flour of dubious quality, eggs, sugar and margarine. Opongo took on the role of an electric whisk to mix it all together! The mixture was then poured into a cake tin and then put into the 'Camp oven'. This consisted of a sufria, a large aluminium saucepan with no handles and a lid, into which we put the cake tin. We wrapped towels around it so as to insulate the pot and put a coat on the top then carefully placed the sufria on the hot coals.

To our immense amazement and joy the cake actually rose and after cutting it and filling the middle with jam and our buttercream, it tasted surprisingly good and the guests were duly impressed.

Another kitchen incident of which I bear a scar was that I was merrily slicing carrots with one of those magical sharp gadgets, and almost sliced off the tip of my little finger! I had some primitive first aid, bandaged it up with a serviette and carried on preparing the salad. On return from his game drive, Mike tended to my finger which proved to be more painful than actually cutting it! With my finger now properly bandaged I could carry on with the campsite tasks.

After five days I left the Mara to return with the clients to Nairobi by air where I met up with my Mum and Aunty Liz who had arrived from the UK for a short holiday in Kenya. We then took Aunty Liz on safari, so back to the Mara for me and although I was tired from working there so recently, we had a wonderful time and this time I was playing the role of a client, hey this was luxury, but I felt I'd earned it!

We stayed at one of the more permanent camps in the Mara that happened to be managed by Charlie Davis, a close family friend, so were extremely well looked after. One morning an interesting event happened. Our early morning tea and biscuits had been left on the tent veranda when the local baboons decided that the biscuits were too good to miss and made off with some of them. You would have laughed at the sight of me, frantically waving my arms in an effort to chase them away before they pinched the lot!

Two bull elephants blocking the road

Lion on a termite mound

Flying Jackie up to a 21st Birthday Party

We had been invited to a 21st birthday party of a friend who lived 'up country', which meant North of Nairobi and in this instance the gathering was on a farm near Mount Kenya. Friends of ours owned an airstrip nearby and as we had two options getting to the party one, a 4- or 5-hour drive or two the other was for me to fly Jackie and I up to

CHAPTER EIGHT

Timau and the Fernandes farm strip. Well, as you can imagine as a recently qualified pilot and with this as an option the later was most definitely the one we took.

Once out of controlled airspace around the Wilson, the Military Airbase and Jomo Kenyatta International Airport (JKIA) all of which were in very close proximity to Nairobi, it was a case of self-navigation over the hills and up country. In Kenya there were some great and very obvious navigation features which helped to keep you on track.

The party was great fun, and went on to late in the night with lots of dancing and drinking but as I had to fly back the next day, discipline and common sense prevailed.

I had pre-prepared my route back to Wilson airport and this included flying through the air corridor between the Military airbase and JKIA. This was the equivalent of flying through an invisible funnel not veering off course too far otherwise you would interfere with Commercial planes coming in or military air activity. Had I done either it could have resulted in serious consequences for me.

We set off in clear weather from Timau and all was going well until we reached the high ground just before the land dropped away towards the funnel. The cloud was low and the ground was hilly and high, the gap was narrowing and it was one of those situations where the visibility was poor. I knew where I was headed and everything was fine except this cloud. In normal circumstances, as in much of the flying I had been doing,

The highlands between Nairobi and Mt Kenya

I would have had Dad in the right-hand seat and would have been able to draw on his experience and advice. But, now all of a sudden it was Jackie sitting next to me in blissful ignorance, admiring the view! In the meantime, my mind was working overtime, doing various calculations, working out my options and trying to decide whether to push on or turn back. If I turned back what were my options? It was certainly one of those situations where I knew enough to get into trouble but maybe not enough to get out of trouble.

However, all ended happily, I stuck to my guns, concentrated and pulled everything I had learned together and fortunately for me, the gap in the cloud was just enough to get me out and away from the high ground with its cloud. I don't recall letting Jackie know how tense the situation had been but as we survived and there was no need to tell her!

Helping out on School expeditions

As Ian Munro, who led most of the expeditions, had left the school I was asked if I would help and assist on the organisational side of preparing expeditions and trips. It was strange but never-the-less very interesting to be doing this and having to take responsibility but worth it, as I could share what I had learnt during my days at school.

I also helped in running trips for other schools and it was such fun to be considered

the 'guru'! Showing others, the ropes, finding caves, instructing them on rock climbing techniques together with safety and general self-awareness that you need when in the bush and the harsh African environment, was very satisfying. Trips included; Longonot & Hells Gate, caving in Mt Suswa, climbing at Lukenya and navigation around Olorgesailie. Olorgesailie is a pre-historic site world renown as the "factory of stone tools" about an hour's drive from Nairobi towards Lake Magadi. It is a very hot dry and arid place.

Ewaso Nyiro & the 'Safari Surgeons'

Sometimes we would just go camping with a bunch of friends but occasionally there was a reason for doing so. This time it was a bird counting safari and the region our group had responsibility for was around the Ewaso Nyiro (meaning Brown River) which lies West of Lake Magadi.

CHAPTER EIGHT

On this adventure, as with many others we went on was with Robin and Biddy Davis, both larger than life characters in the Kenyan community. Robin was fondly known as 'Father Davis' and came complete with green land cruiser, deer hunter hat, his wonky arthritic fingers and tackies (trainers) with holes made to accommodate his equally wonky toes plus big baggy shorts and allegedly without underpants!

Biddy, not surprisingly was known as 'Mother Davis'. She was an amazing lady with a big heart and passionate about her horses, dogs and cows. Biddy was always involved in shows with these animals and instrumental in arranging, hosting and entertaining judges from the respective areas. Mother and Father Davis often invited the judges to join us on our mad safaris to give them the 'full Kenyan experience'!

As I mentioned in earlier chapters, camping was a very serious business and always done in style. This continued throughout my growing up and this trip was no exception. We, as with all campers, knew what the others would normally take and so only a short exchange of details was needed to ensure that all aspects were covered to provide luxury while away. We normally used the big green canvas tents which were large enough to stand up in and to put proper camp beds which meant we were off the ground and away from snakes and scorpions. Someone, normally Robin and Biddy

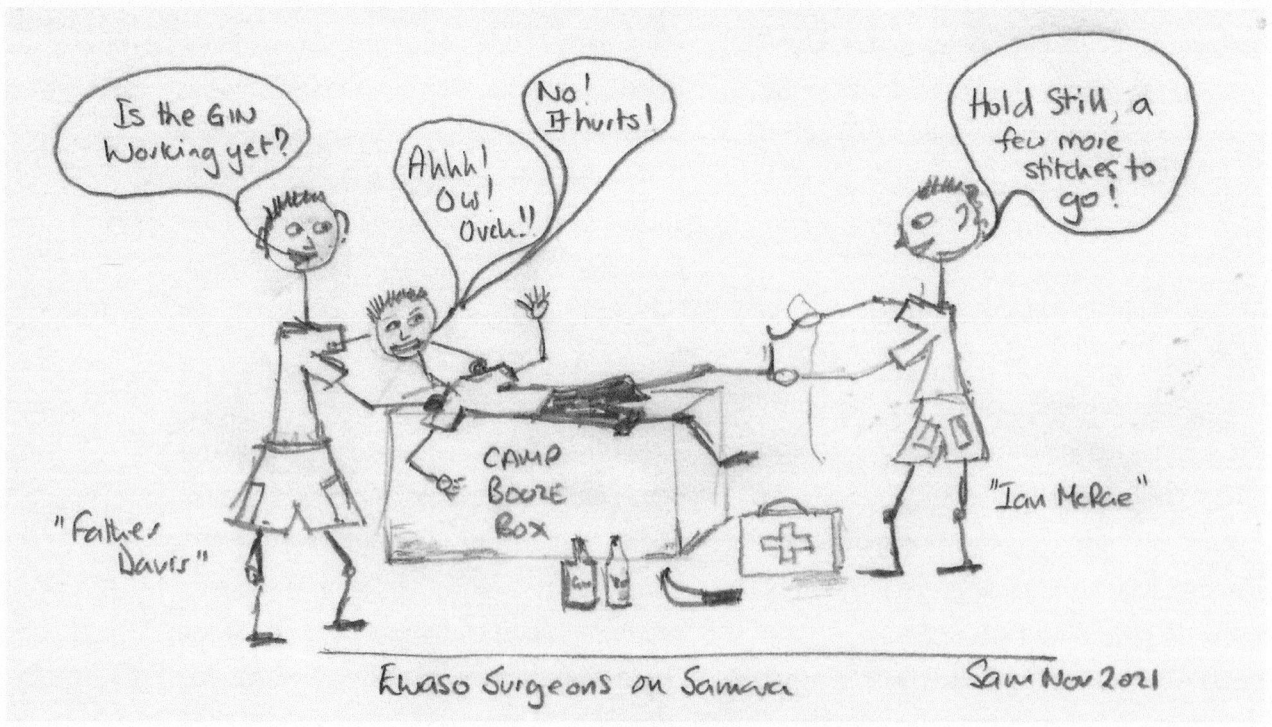

provided the tent that became the mess tent or kitchen tent and the awning to go with it creating shade. Often 'Mother and Father' even brought their pishi (cook) if there were lots of us as well as the kitchen sink!

This campsite was on the bank of the Ewaso Nyiro River, which doubled up as a convenient fridge or method of keeping the beers and sodas cooler than in the air. We had all got to the campsite and as was the norm everyone set about their tasks in setting up camp. I had headed off into the bundu (bush) armed with a panga (sharp bush knife) to collect firewood and clear some of the shrub to make pathways to tend areas and toilet zones. Once my task was done, I heading back to the main area casually swinging my arms, panga in hand and in doing so inadvertently drove the pointed end into my leg, oops! Well, I didn't feel much to start off with but then the warm sensation of blood dribbling down my ankle and then my flip flop becoming slippery made me take a look! Hmmm, I thought I'd better tell someone. Well, 'Mother Davis' was seated in the central area issuing instructions so I passed on my news to her. Pretty quickly 'Father' was called and then Ian McRae, another regular camper with our group, was summoned. Mum appeared when she became aware of the commotion and realised, I was involved, saw the blood then went all wobbly herself so had to sit down and was of no further help to the situation apart from providing the gin.

Horizontal bird spotting

Basic first aid in the form of applied pressure to stop the bleeding, raising the leg and sitting down while 'Father' and Ian scrummaged around in their first aid bags to see what they might have between them to 'fix' the gash. 'Father Davis' found a suture needle (surgical needle) albeit a bit rusty and cat gut or fishing line. Anyway, a bit of filing of the rust and sterilising the needle with the flame of a lighter sorted that problem out.

Next was to clean the wound which had

CHAPTER EIGHT

been made from a dirty panga into skin that was dusty and dirty, so the risk of infection quite high. We were all up to speed on our tetanus jabs. Funnily enough there were no alcohol wipes in the rarely used first aid collections, however, there was vodka in the drinks box so a bit of this was rationed out for giving the fairly deep cut a good scrubbing! This was not the most comfortable experience I can tell you, but as I was told repeatedly it just needed doing and as there was no anaesthetic or method of numbing the area either, it was fortunate we travelled with a good stock of alcohol on safari and now a good swig of near neat Gin was administered, purely for medicinal purposes of course!

I can't quite remember where I was positioned but certainly high enough for the stitching operation to commence and really this was an eye watering experience despite the gin. Mum was being kept out of the way and it was decided that 'Father' and his wonky fingers would hold me down to keep me as still as possible while Ian McRae took on the role of the chief surgeon! After much tugging, some cursing and quite a few squeals and squeaks from me the job was done. I vaguely remember 4 or 5 stitches then a bandage and a couple of pairs of socks in an attempt to keep the African dust out of the wound. Don't forget we had not long arrived and we certainly did not want to be going back to Nairobi, which would have spoilt the fun.

The rest of the safari was spent keeping my leg dry and away from dirt and dust.

However, the Safari surgeons had done an amazing job as the gash healed well, and to this day only a small but very neat scar is left to show and remind me of this adventure.

Closing lines

I have now finished my story of growing up in Kenya and the happy childhood I enjoyed. This, as I said in the beginning, was due to the fact I had wonderful loving parents who cared for us deeply.

Chapter Nine
DAD'S ACCIDENT

AT THE BEGINNING OF Chapter Seven, I said that whilst flying has given me enormous pleasure and fun, it has also provided me with one of the greatest losses in my life; "The Death of my Father".

I was back in Kenya in 1991 for summer holidays after a year in the UK and got involved in the Annual Air Show that was being held, by helping on the committee etc and generally making myself useful. Dad was always very much involved in the Show and he had been on the Committee for years and always took part in many of the events.

The Pegasus Flyers flypast, the various competitions, running the heats to get to the finals was all part of Dad's involvement. He also produced competitions to entertain spectators by doing aerobatics displays.

It was standard procedure to practice the day before. Saturday was practice day and most events were rehearsed then. One of these was a race between a Rally Car and an Aeroplane with both starting at the end of the runway together. The idea being, to do three laps of the course, turning at the first taxiway and then back down the runway. The car is fastest to start with but after 3 laps it gets closer and, in the end, could go either way.

On this particular Saturday, I flew in one of the planes belonging to Pegasus Flyers to practice the opening formation flypast and then completed a competition practice run with Dad and it was then he decided to practice the car vs aeroplane race.

I remember wanting to go with him, but as he was doing this in a new type of aircraft, he suggested it would be best not to. So he dropped me off and I sat on the platform to watch. They started off at the end of the runway as usual, the first run being the most difficult as you start low and slow which is what went terribly wrong. He crashed because he didn't have enough height to pull out of the turn. I couldn't believe my eyes. In fact, I still find it hard to believe, a slow-motion moment that is somehow detached from you. There was no fire, just sudden silence, I walked back into the Aero Club with someone and from there it was so surreal almost a blur. Mum was at home with my brother David, 13, my sister Jackie was on a polo tour in the UK. I don't remember any major dramas as the outcome was quite clear. Dad was dead!

The Air Show was the next day and Mum and I decided that it should continue regardless, as it would have been what Dad wanted. I can only describe my desire to carry on flying. There was no nervousness, and much like falling off a horse, the best thing to do was to get back on, and having had many falls, that is exactly what I did. I flew in the opening flypast of the Show with a safety pilot and I felt as if Dad was there talking me through what I needed to do. I felt quite confident, I carried on with whatever tasks I had been given to do on the day and flew again in the final flypast which was a tribute to Dad. I took my brother David up with me and a couple of other passengers, I don't think there was much emotion. I just did it.

When I look back now through my log book, I flew quite a lot in the days that followed before I returned to the UK to start my second year at University and to join the Air Squadron. It must have been the medicine I needed and the upbringing I had been given that gave me the strength to carry on. Dad died doing what he loved doing, it was his passion, he had passed his passion on to me and the thing he would have hated most would have been for me to stop. I read at his memorial service a passage "You Cannot Die" and do tend to use this as my strength. Dad was an opportunity taker and he very much passed that on to me as often he would say, you only get an opportunity once so take it.

GLOSSARY

Askari
Night watchman/guard

Ayah
House girl/maid/childminder

Banda
Small basic building for accommodation (in national parks)

Bundu bashing
Pushing and cutting your way through the thorny bush/shrub land

Dukas
Small shop

Kiosk
Temporary wooden stall, locals sell their goods at

Lugga
A dry river bed that is prone to flash flooding.

Matatu
A crowded minibus taxi, renowned for high-speed breath-taking travel

Mbwa kali
Dangerous dog

Murram road
Dirt road

Nyama choma
Cooked/burnt meat

Shamba girl
A gardener

Sufria
Large aluminium saucepan/cooking pot with no handles but comes with a flat lid

Syce
Groom or helper with horses

Vlei
Low-lying, marshy ground, covered with water during the rainy season

Printed in Great Britain
by Amazon